Second Edition

An Introduction to
Culture
and Tourism

문화관광영어

이승재 편저

BAEKSAN
Publishing Co.

'문화'는 21세기 최대 화두이며, '관광' 또한 20세기부터 체계화되기 시작하여 21세기에 본격적으로 학문의 궤도에 오르면서 발전하고 있는 신학문으로 창조경제의 한 축을 구성하고 있는 신성장 동력산업이다.

문화와 관광은 직조물(fabric)의 날실과 씨실처럼 불가분의 관계를 이루고 있으며, 이를 전달하는 매체(mediator)인 영어는 문화와 관광산업에서 필수적인 요소이다. 따라서 문화, 관광, 그리고 영어는 21세기 환대산업을 이해하는데 꼭 필요한 3대 분야라고 할 수 있다.

이 책에서는 문화와 관광이라는 친숙하면서도 정의하기 어려운 두 분야를 중심으로 각각의 개념을 소개하고, 이 두 분야의 접합점으로 관광지와 문화이벤트 등을 소개했다. 또한 관광학의 입문서로서 향후 직업가능성에 대해서도 간략히 소개하면서 마무리하였다.

다양한 학문과 연관된 다제학문으로서의 환대산업인 '관광'을 체계적이고 포괄적인 시각으로 이해하는데 조금이나마 도움이 되었으면 하는 마음에서 본서를 편집하였으며, 기꺼이 출판을 도와주신 백산출판사에 심심한 감사를 드린다.

이 승 재

CONTENTS

Part VI — Attractions and Cultural Events

Part VII — Perspectives in Tourism

APPENDIX

Tourism

1

Tourism Overview

Theobald (1994) suggested that etymologically, the word "tour" is derived from the Latin 'tornare' and the Greek 'tornos,' meaning 'a lathe or circle; the movement around a central point or axis.' This meaning has been changed in modern English to represent 'one's turn.' Therefore, like a circle, a tour represents a journey that is a round trip, i.e., the act of leaving and then returning to the original starting point, and therefore, one who takes such a journey can be called a tourist.

Tourism has become a popular global leisure activity. It is commonly associated with trans-national travel, but may also refer to travel to another location within the same country. Tourism is an activity done by an individual or a group of individuals for recreational, leisure or business purposes, which leads to a motion from a place to another.

Tourism has become a popular global leisure activity as well as a major source of income for many countries, and it affects the economy of both the source and host countries.[1] Tourism encompasses all providers of visitor

---

1) In 2012, international tourist arrivals surpassed the milestone 1 billion tourists globally for the first time in history. International tourism receipts (the travel item of the balance of payments) grew to US$1.03 trillion (€740 billion) in 2011, corresponding to an increase in real terms of

and visitor-related services, and it is vital for many countries, due to the large intake of money for businesses with their goods and services and the bulk of employment opportunity in the service industries associated with tourism.

The tourism industry, often referred to as the hospitality industry, encompasses the global industry of travel, attractions, lodging and transportation as well as related components, such as food and entertainment, that meet the needs and wants of tourists traveling away from home. Hospitality is a service based industry, and it is a composite of activities, services, and industries that deliver a travel experience. These service industries include **transportation services**, such as airlines, cruise ships and taxis, **hospitality services**, such as accommodations, including hotels and resorts, and catering such as restaurants, and **entertainment venues**, such as amusement parks, casinos, shopping malls, various music venues and the theatre.

Vocabulary

• etymologically	• derive	• composite
• intake	• hospitality	• encompass
• providers	• tourist	• components
• consecutive	• remunerate	• venues

Comprehension

1. What is the origin of the term "tour"? Where does the term "tour" originate from?
2. What is hospitality industry?
3. Which components consist of hospitality industry?

3.8% from 2010. (Wikipedia)

Definition of Tourism

Tourism may be defined as the sum of the phenomena and relationships arising from the interaction of tourists, business suppliers, host governments, and host communities in the process of attracting and hosting these tourists and other visitors. To define tourism must consider the various groups that participate in and are affected by this industry. Four perspectives — the tourists, the businesses providing tourist goods and services, the government of the host community and the host community — are vital to the development of a comprehensive definition[2] (partly excerpt from McIntosh & Goeldner 1995:10).

In 1941, Hunziker and Krapf defined tourism as "the sum of the

---

2) ① The tourist. The tourist seeks various psychic and physical experiences and satisfactions. The nature of these will largely determine the destinations chosen and the activities enjoyed.

② The businesses providing tourist goods and services. Business people see tourism as an opportunity to make a profit by supplying the goods and services that the tourist market demands.

③ The government of the host community or area. Politicians view tourism as a wealth factor in the economy of their jurisdictions.

④ The host community. Local people usually see tourism as a cultural and employment factor. Of importance to this group is the effect of the interaction between large numbers of international visitors and residents. This effect may be beneficial or harmful, or both.

phenomena and relationships arising from the travel and stay of non-residents, insofar as they do not lead to permanent residence and are not connected with any earning activity". In 1976, the Tourism Society of England's definition was: "Tourism is the temporary, short-term movement of people to destination outside the places where they normally live and work and their activities during the stay at each destination. It includes movements for all purposes." In 1981, the International Association of Scientific Experts in Tourism defined tourism in terms of particular activities selected by choice and undertaken outside the home. (en.wikipedia.org) The International Conference on Travel and Tourism Statistics convened by the World Tourism Organization (WTO) in Ottawa, Canada, in 1991 finally reviewed, updated, and expanded the definition of tourism on the work of earlier definitions of tourism.

Tourism

WTO has taken the concept of *tourism* beyond a stereotypical image of "holiday-making." The officially accepted definition is: "Tourism comprises the activities of persons traveling to and staying in places outside their usual environment for not more than one consecutive year for leisure, business and other purposes." The term 'usual environment' is intended to exclude trips within the area of usual residence, the frequent and regular trips between the domicile and the workplace, and other community trips of a routine character (excerpted from UNWTO).

Classification of Travel Forms

The United Nations classifies three forms of tourism in 1994, in its "Recommendations on Tourism Statistics"; **Domestic tourism**, which involves residents of the given country traveling only within this country; **Inbound tourism**, involving non-residents traveling in the given country; and **Outbound tourism**, involving residents traveling in another country. The UN also derives different categories of tourism by combining the three basic forms of tourism: Internal tourism, which comprises domestic tourism and inbound tourism; National tourism, which comprises domestic tourism and outbound tourism; and International tourism, which consists of inbound tourism and outbound tourism.

Tourists

The World Tourism Organization defines tourists as people who "travel to and stay in places outside their usual environment for more than twenty-four hours and not more than one consecutive year for leisure, business and other purposes not related to the exercise of an activity remunerated from within the place visited".[UNWTO]

Vocabulary

- perspectives
- inbound tourism
- residents
- host
- outbound tourism
- domicile routine
- classify

Comprehension

1. What is WTO short for? What does WTO stand for?
2. When defining tourism, which aspects should be considered?
3. What is the definition of tourism officially adopted by WTO?
4. What is meant by the term "usual environment"?
5. What is the difference between inbound and outbound tourism?
6. What is the difference between internal and domestic tourism?

Discussion

1. Define Tourism in your own way, and explain your reasoning.
   Tourism is _____.
   Because _____.

3

History of Tourism

The subject of travel is exciting and fascinating. Human beings have been moving from place to place for about 1 million years. When we think of tourism, we think primarily of people who are visiting a particular place for sightseeing, visiting friends and relatives, taking a vacation, and having a good time. Although people throughout history have travelled for various reasons, tourism as we know it today - involving large numbers of people travelling mainly for pleasure - is quite a recent phenomenon. Tourism for the masses is a relatively new phenomenon, but many historical documents provide accounts of travel and tourism e.g. various evidences for the nomadic lifestyle in the earliest humans.

Until recently, most travel was done for specific reasons; travels precipitated by the changing seasons that resulted in a depletion of food sources or the need to escape danger. Travel for the purpose of trade can be traced to the Sumerians of Babylonia, about 4000 B.C.[3] As travel evolved,

---

3) The invention of money by the Sumerians (Babylonians) and the development of trade beginning about 4000 B.C. mark the beginning of the modern era of travel. Not only were the Sumerians the first to grasp the idea of money and use it in business transactions, but they were also the first to invent cuneiform writing and the wheel, so they should be credited as the founders of the travel business.

it took on many forms such as peace-making voyages of Queen Hatshepsut in 1480 B.C.[4] Travel was also undertaken for religious purposes described in the Old Testament. In 776 B.C. with the first Olympic Games, came one of the earliest forms of planned attractions.

During the Roman Republic, travel outside a person's local area for leisure was largely confined to wealthy classes. Medicinal spas and coastal resorts such as Baiae were popular for the rich. By the middle Ages, traditions of pilgrimage motivated even the lower classes to undertake distant journeys for health or spiritual improvement. Modern tourism can be traced to what was known as the Grand Tour, which was a traditional trip around Europe, (especially Germany and Italy), undertaken by mainly upper-class European young men of means, mainly from Western and Northern European countries.[5] It served as an educational opportunity and rite of passage (partly excerpted from en.wikipedia.org).

As the examples show, the travel in early times was hard work, which is validated by the etymology; it was no coincidence that travel and travail have the same root word. Our ancestors did not think that the word "travel" was synonymous with the word "pleasure," as so many of us does today. Travel was difficult and dangerous and only undertaken for reasons of necessity.

---

4) Probably the first journey ever made for purposes of peace and tourism was made by Queen Hatshepsut to the lands of Punt (believed to be on the east coast of Africa) in 1480 B.C.E. Descriptions of this tour have been recorded on the walls of the Temple of Deir El Bahari at Luxor. These texts and bas reliefs are among the world's rarest artworks and are universally admired for their wondrous beauty and artistic qualities.

5) The custom flourished from about 1660 until the advent of large-scale rail transit in the 1840s, and was associated with a standard itinerary. The tradition was extended to include more of the middle class after rail and steamship travel made the journey less of a burden, and Thomas Cook made the "Cook's Tour" a byword.

Vocabulary

- sightseeing
- depletion
- synonymous
- nomadic lifestyle
- etymology
- rite of passage
- precipitate
- coincidence

Comprehension

1. Why do people travel?
2. What is Mass Tourism?
3. What were the reasons for making people move in the past?
4. Travel is synonymous with the word _____ today.
5. _____ has the same root with 'travail.'
6. What was the first form of journey made for peace?
7. What were the main characteristics of journeys in the past?
8. What changes occurred to travel in Roman Republic?
9. What was the form of travel in the Middle Ages?
10. What is Grand Tour?

Discussion

1. With a partner, share your experience of traveling. Elaborate on your reasons for travelling.
2. Who is Queen Hatshepsut?
3. Summarize the history of tourism in English.

Four Components of Tourism

The tourism industry is comprised of thousands of companies whose primary purpose is to provide services and products for tourists. The companies involved are as varied as they are numerous and include everything from "mom and pop" diners to multi-national corporations.

There are four basic components of the tourism industry. The four components are attractions, transportation, accommodation and food and beverage. The combined efforts of these four components make it possible, even desirable, for people to travel.

1. Attractions

People travel for many different reasons. Some travel because of business obligations, while others travel for pleasure. Those traveling for pleasure usually travel to visit relatives or to experience new and different attractions around the world. A tourist attraction is a place of interest where tourists visit, typically for its inherent or exhibited natural or cultural value, historical significance, natural or built beauty, offering leisure, adventure and amusement (wikipedia). Attractions are what draw individuals to specific destinations, and are often called as tourist destinations. "They may be based on natural resources, culture, ethnicity or entertainment" (Miller 1990).

Natural resources such as beaches, mountains and forests, are examples of traditional tourist attractions. Tourists have always traveled to natural areas of beauty to seek solace from their everyday lives. This type of tourism is called ecotourism. Ecotourism is a type of environmentally oriented tourism in which tourist from around the globe seek out natural wonders (Fridgen 1991).[6] Other examples of cultural tourist attractions include historical places, monuments, ancient temples, theme parks and ethnic communities or cultural events.

Man-made attractions range from the Pyramids in Egypt and the Incan ruins in Peru to Disney World in Florida. With the overwhelming success of both Disneyland[7] and Disney World, there has been a flourish of imitators developed to provide tourists with the excitement they are seeking at theme parks.

Gaming has also become a major player in the tourism industry. Las Vegas,[8] Nevada has made tourism the number one industry in the state.

---

6) The U.S. National Park System attracted 9 million foreign visitors, which is more than 20 percent of the total foreign visitors to the country. There are over 1,100 national parks and 3,200 nature preservations across the world. Many undeveloped areas are studying ways to capitalize on their natural resources without changing or destroying the natural beauty.

7) To all who come to this happy place: Welcome. Disneyland is your land. Here age relives fond memories of the past, and here youth may savor the challenge and promise of the future. Disneyland is dedicated to the ideals, the dreams, and the hard facts that have created America, with the hope that it will be a source of joy and inspiration to all the world. — Walter E. Disney

8) Over 36 million visitors and convention attendees in 2009 enjoy the lights and sounds of Las

Gone is the misconception that Las Vegas is a "den of iniquity"; Las Vegas is now promoting itself as a family vacation destination. Theme hotels and theme parks are helping the city to entice families there. Gaming is also popular in other parts of the world as well as on cruise ships.

📖 Vocabulary

- mom and pop diners
- multi-national corporations
- destination
- ethnicity
- eco-tourism
- man-made attractions

🎓 Comprehension

1. What is the definition of attractions?
2. To qualify attractions, which aspects should be considered?
3. What is eco-tourism?
4. Think of some examples of eco-tourism.
5. Give some examples of man-made attractions.
6. What is the old notorious nickname of Las Vegas?
7. What is most successful industry in Nevada?

Vegas and the glittering strip. Las Vegas currently has the ten largest resort hotels in the world.

👥 Discussion

1. If you are requested to recommend a national park in your country, which one would it be? And why?

2. If you were to recommend one man-made attraction, which one would it be?

3. Between man-made and natural attractions, which do you prefer?

4. What does the plaque at the entrance of Disneyland say?

2. Transportation

As it was made evident in the discussion of the history of tourism, transportation has been an integral part of the tourism industry; transportation is the main mean to carry passengers, which links tourists with various tourist attractions, where tourism services are performed. There is a general agreement that tourism expands more when there are better transportation systems. The development of transportation, such as transportation vehicles, infrastructure and technological innovations speed up the development of tourism (excerpted from Westlake and Robbins 2005).

The earliest travelers journeyed on foot or horseback in caravans or groups to provide safety and comfort to one another. Means of travel were included on foot, by animals or by ship or boat. The simplest being foot, although horseback improved the pace, walking did not hinder the distance one could travel. Camels, donkeys,

bullocks and elephants were also used whilst travelling. Using animals as transport made the trip both expensive and allowed the traveler to carry more supplies for trade or suchlike. Early sea vessels varied from dugout tree trunks to the complex Roman galleys. As vehicles of travel were invented and fine-tuned, travel became more prominent.

Worldwide, domestic tourists generally travel by automobile.[9] The automobile transportation makes it easy to see local culture and nations.

9) In 1990, according to the Federal Highway Administration, Americans traveled more than 2 trillion intercity passenger-miles. Of those 2 trillion miles, 81 percent were by car, while air travel accounted for 17 percent. Rail passenger transportation and motor coach transportation also play an important but smaller role in domestic travel, providing the most support in intracity travel. In 1988, the number of paying passengers was 335.8 billion (Fridgen 1991).

It presents great flexibility in contrast to other modes of transportation (Oter, 2007). When compared with the prices in air transportation, automobile provides price benefits, but the main factor affecting this choice is time and distance.

Air travel has revolutionized the tourism industry. Today air travel is not only reasonably priced, but easy to make access by a phone call or the on-line booking service on any of major carriers to almost anywhere in the world. The primary advantage of air travel is the speed in which the traveler can reach his or her destination: in a relatively short period of time (5~6 hours), an individual can fly from coast to coast. The airlines now make it possible for people to travel to faraway destination in short periods of time — this supports the new trend of tourism, more frequent but shorter vacations. The airlines have also provided easy access for business travelers to their many business meetings and conferences.

The other mode that affects tourism is railway transportation. This type of transportation was frequently used in 19th century. But nowadays application of technology and technological innovation gave birth to fast trains which compete with air and automobile transportation modes.

The cruise in sea transportation has a special place in tourism. Named as sailing hotels, this type of transportation provides tourists with the opportunity to see several countries at a time, and it is the most expensive one.

From direct, efficient air travel to luxury cruise ships, transportation experiences often set the tone for travel and leave impressions that can last a lifetime. 17% of tourism employees work in Transportation in British Columbia.

Vocabulary

- domestic tourists
- caravans
- intercity
- intracity
- rail passenger transportation
- motor
- coach transportation
- air travel
- automobile

Comprehension

1. What is the most vital component to the success of the tourism industry?
2. How did the earliest travelers travel?
3. According to the Federal Highway Administration, what is the major mode of travel for domestic travel?
4. Why is it said that air travel has revolutionized the tourism industry?
5. What is the primary advantage of air travel?

3. Accommodation

Travel also requires accommodation: tourists needed places to sleep and take nourishment. To accommodate the new demand for travel (many of the earliest travelers were religious individuals), inns were provided. Accommodations for travelers go back into antiquity, and various historical accounts of roadside inns and lodging facilities have been found: it is the world's oldest commercial business. The early lodging facilities rendered lodging for both the travelers and their animals.[10]

Accommodation is one of the largest and fastest growing sectors in the tourism industry now.[11] People traveling needed a place to sleep; the lodging industry is an extremely important component of the tourism industry. Lodging encompasses a broad spectrum of supplier businesses; accommodation categories can include hotels, motels, conference centers, inns, bed and breakfasts, resort condominiums, youth hostels, and health spas. The type of hotel is determined primarily by the size and location of the building structure, and then by the function, target market, service level, other amenities, and industry standards.

---

10) They provided fresh horses, and lodgings were available for rent to visitors when they arrived at their destination.

11) According to the American Hotel and Motel Association (AH&MA), the lodging industry enjoyed its most successful and profitable year in 1997, and expectations are that performance will be strong through the remainder of the decade. The industry numbered 3.8 million rooms and $85.6 billion in sales in 1997.

4. Hotels[12)]

The word *hotel* is derived from the French *hôtel* (coming from the same origin as *hospital*), which referred to a French version of a building seeing frequent visitors, and providing care, rather than a place offering accommodation. In contemporary French usage, *hôtel* now has the same meaning as the English term.

A **hotel** is an establishment that provides lodging paid on a short-term basis. Facilities provided may range from a basic bed and storage for clothing, to luxury features like en-suite bathrooms. Facilities offering hospitality to travelers have been a feature of the earliest civilizations. In Greco-Roman, culture hospitals for recuperation and rest were built at thermal baths. During the middle Ages, various religious orders at monasteries and abbeys would offer accommodation for travelers on the road.

The precursor to the modern hotel was the inn of medieval Europe, possibly dating back to the rule of Ancient Rome.[13)] Famous London examples of inns include the George and the Tabard.[14)] Inns began to cater for richer clients in the mid-18th century, and consequently grew in grandeur and the level of service provided. One of the first hotels in a modern sense was opened in Exeter in 1768, but hotels proliferated throughout Western Europe and North America in the 19th century. Luxury hotels, including Tremont House and Astor House in the United States, Savoy Hotel in the United Kingdom and the Ritz chain of hotels in London and Paris, began to spring up in the later part of the century, catering to an extremely wealthy clientele. (excerpted from en.wikipedia.org)

Hotel operations vary in size, function, and cost. Most hotels and major hospitality companies have set industry standards to classify hotel types.[15)]

---

12) Grammatically, hotels usually take the definite article – hence "The Astoria Hotel" or simply "The Astoria."

13) These would provide for the needs of travelers, including food and lodging, stabling and fodder for the traveler's horse(s) and fresh horses for the mail coach.

14) A typical layout of an inn had an inner court with bedrooms on the two sides, with the kitchen and parlor at the front and the stables at the back.

15) **An upscale full-service hotel facility** offers luxury amenities, full service accommodations,

The WTO estimates that the world hotel room inventory grows by about 2.5 percent a year.[16] Occupancy rates vary, but they average about 65 percent overall. Employment possibilities[17] are growing for accelerated career advancement, and opportunities for positions in differing regions and types of establishments are also expanding.

Most hotel establishments consist of a General Manager who serves as the head executive (often referred to as the "Hotel Manager"), department heads who oversee various departments within a hotel, middle managers, administrative staff, and line-level supervisors. The organizational chart and volume of job positions and hierarchy varies by hotel size, function, and is often determined by hotel ownership and managing companies.

Vocabulary

- lodging facility
- revenue
- recuperation
- accommodation
- nourishment
- thermal baths
- supplier business
- occupancy rate
- precursor • proliferate

Comprehension

1. Where were the earliest lodging facilities located?
2. Who were the earliest travelers?
3. What is the lodging industry?
4. What are included in the accommodation categories?

---

on-site full service restaurant(s), and the highest level of personalized service. **Full service hotels** often contain upscale full-service facilities with a large volume of full service accommodations, on-site full service restaurant(s), and a variety of on-site amenities. **Boutique hotels** are smaller independent non-branded hotels that often contain upscale facilities. **Small to medium-sized hotel** establishments offer a limited amount of on-site amenities. **Economy hotels** are small to medium-sized hotel establishments that offer basic accommodations with little to no services. **Extended stay hotels** are small to medium-sized hotels that offer longer term full service accommodations compared to a traditional hotel.(wikipedia)

16) In 1994 the WTO estimated that there were about 12.2 million rooms worldwide.

17) In 1997, approximately 173,000 workers were employed in hotels and other lodging operations in Canada.

5. What is the first form of lodging?

👥 Discussion

1. What kind of lodging do you use most when you travel?
2. Briefly summarize the developmental stages of accommodation industry.

5. The Food and Beverage

The food and beverage sector is a vibrant and multifaceted part of tourism, and is commonly known as **F&B**. **Foodservice** (US English) or **catering industry** (British English) defines those businesses, institutions, and companies responsible for any meal prepared outside the home. This industry includes restaurants, school and hospital cafeterias, catering operations, and many other formats (en. wikipedia.org). **Beverages** or **drinks** are liquids, specifically prepared for human consumption. In addition to basic needs, beverages form a part of the culture of human society.

Like the lodging industry, the food service industry is a very old business. Such service came out of the early inns and monasteries. Eating and drinking are favorite pastimes of travelers, and the food service industry would face difficult times without the tourist market. This sector encompasses all types of establishments supplying food and beverages for consumption, from fine dining specialties, ethnic restaurants and institutional food outlets to catering firms, pubs and lounges.

The industry currently employed more than 9 million people. The National Restaurant Association,[18] a full-service trade association with over 20,000 members is the most important trade association in the food service field.

Vocabulary

- fast-food units
- pastimes
- institutional food
- specialty restaurants
- abbreviation
- establishments
- ethnic restaurants

---

18) The National Restaurant Association (NRA) is the largest foodservice trade association in the world supporting nearly 500,000 restaurant businesses. In 1998, those food industry sales for the year would total $336.4 billion, 4.7percent over 1997. According to the Restaurant Industry Forecast 2014, restaurant-industry sales are expected to hit a record high of $683.4 billion in 2014. (NRA)

🎓 Comprehension

1. What is the NRA?
2. Give some examples of the food service establishments.

👥 Discussion

1. What do you usually eat when you're traveling?
2. What kind of food service establishments do you use the most when you're traveling?

Travel Information

1

Types of Travel

Travelers can be categorized based on the activities what they are doing in their travel, or which methods they take for planning, etc. Types of travel based on the activities are generally categorized into loungers, sightseers, and adventurers. Another categorization based on the travel method is a trailblazer, a so-called F.I.T., or a member of an escorted tour.[1]

1. Loungers, Sightseers, or Adventurers

Loungers[2] might be one of the slowest forms of travel possible, and the

---

1) One study of American tourists, performed by Canada (Rusk: 1974) segmented them into six cluster, each containing individuals with similar vacationing characteristics: Nonactive visitor (29%) seeks familiar surroundings and places he can visit friends and relatives. The active city visitor (12%) seeks familiar surroundings and friends and relatives. Family sightseers (6%) look for places that would be rewarding for children as well as adults. The outdoor vacationers (19%) seek clean air, rest, and quiet in beautiful scenery. Resort vacationers (8%) are most interested in water sports and good weather. Foreign travel vacationers (26%) look for exotic settings for exciting and enriching experiences.

2) The definition of the word 'lounger' is a noun meaning ① a comfortable chair or couch; an extendable chair or a lightweight, usually adjustable, couch designed to be comfortable for the

extended stay. They spent hours walking the streets and observing the lives of those going through their daily routines or the environment. The sightseer is synonymous to tourist who is visiting sights of interest. Tour guides generally bring sightseers to various parts of attractions. Adventure travel[3] is a type of tourism, involving exploration or travel to remote, exotic and possibly hostile areas.

2. Trailblazers, F.I.T.s, or Escorted tours.

As a trailblazer[4] (a term coined for convenience), you'd be completely on your own. This is most important: you should make sure every routing, date, transportation, booking, and hotel reservation before your departure from your country. If you already know your destination well, you'll probably have a wonderful holiday. But if this is your first trip abroad, you're almost bound to run into certain headaches, and disappointments. In off season it's relatively easy, but in today's high season rat race, particularly in the popular tourist spots, the well-meaning but fumbling amateur is often licked before he starts.

The F.I.T. ("Foreign Independent Trip/ Traveler") is ideal for the first-time or unsure new vacationer who wants freedom of movement combined with expert protection. You pick a travel agent, and tell him/her destination, duration, and financial situation for the expedition. The agent will then hand you a tailor-made itinerary that lists dates, times, flight and train numbers, hotels, transfers, the works, and a book of voucher coupons.[5]

As a member of an escorted tour, the third choice, you don't even have to know, for example, Paris is in France or Matterhorn isn't a tuba. It's that simple. If you're a stranger to your destination, or if you're lonely, lazy,

---

user ② somebody who lounges around: somebody who sits or walks in a casual relaxed way (encarta.com).

3) Adventures tourism is rapidly growing in popularity, as tourists seek different kinds of vacations. This may include activities such as mountaineering, trekking, bungee jumping, mountain biking, rafting, zip-lining and rock climbing. (wikipedia)

4) a person who marks a trail through wilderness areas

5) At each airport or station, you will have a friendly face greet you and take over your burdens. If you pay a percentage more, the professional experts will guard your interests.

gregarious, fun-loving, or shy — any of 10-dozen reasons — here might be the perfect answer for your requirements. Parties run from 10~15 to 30~40 or more, with 25 about average. When you sign up, a lump sum must be paid in advance. This usually takes care of the entire trip[6] except your personal use.

It can be a beautifully serene way to go, because all of your problems are supposed to be solved by an experienced third party the company official called 'a tour conductor' in charge of the group. Everything is arranged, down to your last Mona Lisa and your 16th seat from the right in the dining room.

Scores of agencies specialize in this field of travel. Prices vary. If you pick the right operator, you can enjoy more under better conditions for less money than you could possibly do alone-a bargain which no individual tourist could touch.

Vocabulary

- off-season
- routing
- vacationer
- tour conductor
- agency

- high season
- fumbling
- itinerary
- porter
- operator

- destination
- expedition
- voucher
- gregarious

Comprehension

1. Types of travel based on the activities are generally categorized into _____ .

2. Types of travel based on the travel method are _____ .

3. Tour guides are generally accompanied and bring _____ to the attractions.

---

6) It includes all kinds of transportation, hotels, all or part of the meals, sightseeing fees — everything except your tips, wines, liquors, laundry, telephone calls, gambling, gifts, snacks between meals, and others for personal use.

4. _____ involves exploration or travel to remote, exotic and even hostile areas.
5. Who is the trailblazer?
6. What does FIT stand for? And who is a FIT?
7. Explain the escorted tour.
8. Briefly summarize advantages and disadvantages of each category.

👥 Discussion

1. Which type of tourist do you think you are and why?
2. Do you have any experience of being a member of an escorted tour?
3. Where is the Matterhorn? Have you ever visited the Matterhorn?

2
CHAPTER

Travel Document

1. Passport[7]

The passport is a formal document issued by a competent officer of a country to a citizen of the country and now usually necessary for exit from and reentry into the country, that certifies to the identity and citizenship of the bearer, calls upon the officers of foreign governments to extend protection to him when needed, and allows him to travel within the borders of a foreign country when it has been endorsed with a visa by an authorized official of that country. (Webster's 3rd International Dictionary)

The English statement that appears at the front page of the Korean passport reads as follows:

---

7) It is considered unlikely that the term "passport" is derived from sea ports, but rather from a medieval document required to pass through the gate ("porte") of a city wall. (wikipedia)

The Minister of Foreign Affairs and Trade of the Republic of Korea hereby requests all those whom it may concern to permit the bearer, a national of the Republic of Korea, to pass freely without delay or hindrance and, in case of need, to afford him(her) every possible assistance and protection.

The passport as a travel document is not the recent phenomenon. Passports have their origins in the medieval testimonial. In medieval Europe, such documents were issued to travelers by local authorities, and generally contained a list of towns and cities into which a document holder was permitted to pass.[8] King Henry V of England is credited with having invented the first true passport, notwithstanding the earlier examples cited, as a means of helping his subjects prove who they were in foreign lands.[9]

When traveling, the passport is worth more than gold. Don't lend it, or use it as security. If you lose your passport in a foreign country, it makes your itinerary in trouble, pinning you to one spot until the temporary passport is issued. Try to memorize the number of your passport and its date of issuance, for you'll be asked for these facts so many times as you travel.

Vocabulary

• exit	• reentry	• citizenship
• bearer	• endorse	• formality
• security	• nuisance	• authorize
• competent	• issuance	• medieval
• temporary	• testimonial – documents/ statement	

8) A letter from an ecclesiastical superior given to a pilgrim to avoid the latter's possible arrest on charges of vagrancy. Later, papers of authority to travel were more widely issued by the state.

9) Shakespeare (1564-1616) was an English playwright and poet. His birth place is known as Stratford-upon-Avon. Shakespeare's plays are both tragedies (Romeo and Juliet, Hamlet, King Lear, Othello, and Macbeth) and comedies (A Midnight's dream, The Taming of the Shrew, Twelfth Night, and As you Like it). The travel scene in *King Henry V* (Act4: line 3) includes "Let him depart; his passport shall be made."

📝 **Fill in the blank with proper word(s).**

1. The passport is a formal document issued (   ) a competent officer
   of a country (   ) a citizen of the country and now usually
   necessary (   ) exit (   ) and reentry (   ) the country,
   that certifies to the identity and citizenship of the bearer, calls upon
   the officers of foreign governments to extend protection to him when
   needed, and allows him to travel within the borders of a foreign
   country when it has been endorsed with a visa by an authorized official
   of that country.

2. Do you have a passport? How can you obtain it?

3. Explain the actual function of the passport for the bearer.

2. Visa

Visa is one of the formalities necessary in travelling. The day may come when the formalities at borders will disappear, but until then, it is one of the most required official papers.

The word VISA is a surviving fragment of the Latin term 'carta visa' which means "the paper has been seen." It is a stamp of approval put into your passport which declares that this document has been examined and permitted you to enter the county granting the visa. It allows you to stay only for the limited period, so that a passport carries several blank pages marked 'VISA'. You may apply for a visa at the Consulate or Embassy of the country in consideration.

Some country will admit you with only a passport; others ask you to show your passport and a visa; some others forgo both documents in favor of a simple tourist card.[10]

If you travel in Western Europe, for example, your passport is all that's necessary, unless your visit extends beyond several months in any one country. For a longer stay, you will need a visa, just as you will for any visit to the Russia, and China.

📖 Vocabulary

• approval	• fragment	• grant
• forgo: waive, do without	• Consulate	• Embassy

🎓 Comprehension

1. What is the meaning of 'carta visa'?
2. Explain what a VISA is.

---

10) A citizen of a foreign country who seeks to enter the United States (U.S.) generally must first obtain a U.S. visa, which is placed in the traveler's passport, a travel document issued by the traveler's country of citizenship. Certain international travelers may be eligible to travel to the U.S. without a visa if they meet the requirements for visa-free travel. (http://www.travel. state.gov/visa)

3. What is the difference between a Consulate and an Embassy?

4. Which countries need VISA, when you're traveling?

5. In case you stay longer than 6 months in the U.S.A., do you need VISA?

🚻 Discussion

1. Find the word embedding the alphabets '-vis-' in the word as many as possible.

   e.g. visual ······

2. Each country has a different period of stay without having VISA. Find the maximum length of stay without VISA for each country.

   Japan _____ U.S.A. _____

   Canada _____ Thailand _____

3. Quarantine

The quarantine is the formality required visiting foreign countries. The term 'quarantine' came from the old convention of Venice in the 14th century.[11] From this practice have come the English word "quarantine" and the universal recognition, followed down to this day, that governments have the right to protect themselves and their people from epidemic disease.[12]

Today, the Department of Public Health Service requires that travelers be vaccinated depending where they're going, either smallpox, yellow fever, cholera, or other infectious diseases. The purpose of these regulations is to protect you from the serious contagious diseases that still exist in certain parts of the world, and to prevent you, in turn, from carrying them from one country to another. In this demand it is acting in concert with other governments around the world.

Vaccinations should be recorded on an International Certificate of Vaccination form with an "approved stamp" by the local or state health department, and keep it with your passport throughout your trip, ready to show quarantine officers.

Vocabulary

- Quarantine: make somebody resistant to disease by vaccination
- quaranta
- vaccinated
- inoculation
- practice: custom, tradition
- contagious
- immunization
- yellow fever: disease transmitted by mosquitoes
- cholera
- smallpox
- recognition

---

11) The ancient sailors travelling to Venice would not have been able to leave the ship for quaranta or forty days from a port where disease was epidemic, or if someone on your ship was ill. During that time the ship would have lain at anchor (a device to hold a ship in place) in isolation outside the harbor. If, at the end of that siege, everyone was still in good health, the cautious Venetians would have allowed the ship to enter, reassured that no one aboard was infectious.

12) A smallpox vaccination is good for three years, yellow fever for ten, and cholera for six months.

🎓 Comprehension

1. What is the origin of the word "quarantine"?
2. What other words can be used in place of "inoculation"?
3. Find synonyms for the word "epidemic".
4. What are the main purposes of inoculation?

👥 Discussion

1. If you're planning to travel Tanzania, do you need vaccination?
2. Find the word embedding the alphabet series '-quart-' in English.
   e.g. quartet
3. Find some other disease that might be infectious while traveling.

3

Travel Agency

A travel agency is a retail business, that sells travel related products and services to customers, on behalf of suppliers, such as airlines, car rentals, cruise lines, hotels, railways, sightseeing tours and package holidays that combine several products. (en.wikipedia.org) A travel agency is a company treating the tourists and tourism products. The agency acts as a broker, bringing the buyer and seller together. They do not substitute the service-providing unit, but play the role of providing information and access to the visitor and are the middlemen in the purchase of certain services.

A travel agent is an expert working in the travel industry handling the complicated details of arranging travel, e.g. figuring out routes and itineraries, reservations, and costs. When you utilize the services of a travel agent, it often saves time and money.

Travel agents sell the products on a commission basis, paid by the companies they are authorized to represent.[13] They represent a wide variety

---

13) Most travel agencies operate on a commission-basis, meaning that the compensation from the airlines, car rentals, cruise lines, hotels, railways, sightseeing tours and tour operators, etc., is expected in form of a commission from their bookings. Most often, the commission consists of a set percentage of the sale.

of transportation, hotel, and packages in various price brackets. A travel agent is supposed to offer impartial travel advice to the customer: A travel agent knows best how to keep your travel costs down. He/she is also an expert on escorted and independent packaged tours.

Here are several yardsticks of its selection. The first criterion you should look for is membership in such widely recognized organizations as IATA, ASTA,[14] etc.; the second is local reputation; the third is price; the forth is his familiarity with the area he is selling; the fifth is contact with a previous client.

In the United States, American Express and the American Automobile Association (AAA) are examples of mega travel agencies.

Vocabulary

- agent
- utilize: employ
- commission: a sum of money paid to a salesperson for every sale that he/she makes.
- authorize
- client
- yardstick
- criterion
- reputation
- familiarity
- brackets: ranges
- figure out: calculate, compute all the travel details

Comprehension

1. Define a travel agency and a travel agent respectively.
2. What does the travel agent do?
3. Name the most recognized organizations in the travel industry.
4. When you choose a travel agency, what factors do you consider?
5. *The contact of previous clients* can be _____.

---

14) International Air Transport Association (IATA), American Society of Travel Agents (ASTA)

👥 Discussion

1. Name travel agencies in Korea.
2. Choose one of the travel agencies and introduce its business and tour products.

4

CHAPTER

Climate[15)

No one would like to get sodden and damp while sightseeing and even the most fascinating sights lose their enchantment when it's 110 °F in the shade. Knowing the weather at the destination is an important part of your preliminary planning and preparation, and a vital factor in working out your itinerary.

Looking at a map and noting latitudes won't give you much information, for weather depends upon many other factors, including altitude, ocean currents, wind, geographical location, humidity, etc. While temperature is the single most important element in determining how comfortable you will be, all of these factors will influence the weather, and even your mood.

Edinburgh, for example, is as near the North Pole as Moscow, yet the

---

15) Climate encompasses the statistics of temperature, humidity, atmospheric pressure, wind, rainfall, atmospheric particle count and numerous other meteorological elements in a given region over long periods of time. Climate can be contrasted to weather, which is the present condition of these same elements over periods up to two weeks. The climate of a location is affected by its latitude, terrain, altitude, ice or snow cover, as well as nearby water bodies and their currents. Climates can be classified according to the average and typical ranges of different variables, most commonly temperature and precipitation. Köppen climate classification scheme divides the climates into five main groups and several types and subtypes: Tropical, Dry, Temperate, Continental, and Polar climate.

two cities have different climates. London is much farther north than New York, but its winter temperature, like those all over most of northern Europe, are much milder and its summer ones much cooler. Mexico City, which is on the same latitude as Honolulu, has sharper daytime and evening temperature variations because of its altitude and distance from the sea. Similarly, while Quito, Ecuador, is almost on the equator, it is so high in the Andes that its nights are cool. When you make plans below the equator, remember that seasons are the reverse of those above it. In Europe and many other parts of the world, temperatures are read in Centigrade unlike in the U.S.A., where they are read in Fahrenheit. You can convert one into the other by the following formulae:

$$C = (F - 32) \times 5/9 \quad F = C \times 9/5 + 32$$

Vocabulary

- sodden
- preliminary
- altitude
- enchantment: magic, charm
- latitude
- reverse
- currents: a steady and continuous flowing movement of some of the water in a river, lake or sea
- variation: degree of difference
- shade: something that blocks the light
- mood: state of mind
- humidity: moisture content of the atmosphere
- equator: the imaginary circle around the earth; same distance from north pole and south pole
- Centigrade
- Fahrenheit

Comprehension

1. Convert 110°F into Centigrade.
2. Which factors determine the weather?
3. Compare the climate of New York with that of London.

4. Compare the climate of Edinburgh with that of Moscow.
5. Unlike the U.S.A., which temperature systems do the most of European countries use?
6. Which climate zone does Korea belong?
7. Choose the words to describe the weather.

👥 Discussion

1. What is the difference between climate and weather?
2. Do you agree that the weather can have an influence on your mood?
3. Look at the map and make sure each location mentioned in this passage.
4. If you experienced bad weather during your travel, share it with your partner.
5. Find terms to describe the winds.
6. Explain the different temperature systems of Centigrade and Fahrenheit.
7. The capital letter C being the Roman numeral for 100, find other cases to use the capital letter C.

Let us learn more about geographical terms.

5

Luggage

Too much baggage can be a millstone, and overweight charges for excess luggage can mount astronomically on a long trip. Never take more luggage than you can carry yourself: the more experienced traveler, the less he/she is likely to pack. Take what is necessary to your sense of well-being and eliminate all the 'just in case' items — for instance, anything you won't

wear at least three times. Take nothing which you haven't worn pleasantly and comfortably at home, and never take anything brand-new.

Make up your final essential list, and check off items as they go into your suitcase. Here are some tips for packing. Separate hard or bulky things from soft, foldable ones; the clothes for one climate from those for another; the clothes you'll need immediately from those you won't wear for a while; divide all the small items into categories: handkerchiefs, hosiery, etc. Then slip each group into its own plastic envelope, which is waterproof and practically weightless. Tuck little things into the side pockets of your suitcase, so that you can find them easily. Plastic bags in a variety of sizes are very useful not only for various small items but for laundry, a wet bathing suit, etc.

Vocabulary

- millstone
- excess luggage
- make up the list
- separate A from B
- overweight charges
- just in case items
- check off items
- plastic bag

Comprehension

1. When you travel, what would be the best way to pack your baggage?
2. What is a just-in-case item? Give some examples.

Discussion

1. If you have any tips to pack the baggage, share it with your partner.
2. Find the words that can be used for packing.

1. Baggage in the flight

As for the flight passengers, they are required to be at the airport ticket counter to complete necessary departure formalities not later than check-in times shown in the folder. Baggage should be clearly tagged with your name and address. All baggage must be weighed, including overnight bag, briefcase, lady's vanity case, etc, and the total weight should be included in the free baggage allowance. Desk top and cellular phones shall not be operated on board during flight. Only the following articles will be regarded as personal weight and will not be weighed as baggage: a lady's handbag or pocketbook, an overcoat, an umbrella or walking stick, a reasonable amount of reading materials for the flight, an infant's food for consumption en-route, an infant's carrying bassinet, a fully collapsible wheel chair and a pair of crutches.

Vocabulary

- ticket counter
- check-in time
- article
- bassinet

- necessary departure formalities
- tag
- en-route
- crutch(a pair of crutches)

- identify
- collapsible

Comprehension

1. When you check your baggage, what do you do to identify it as yours?
2. Which articles will not be weighed as baggage?

2. Baggage Allowance

All the baggage carried by the passengers should follow the airline's free baggage allowance policy. Baggage allowances are the limits imposed by airlines on luggage amounts that can be stored by passengers. Additional charges may be applied for excess baggage. With the regulations on air travel and baggage allowances changing constantly, you must check the most recent regulations before you take any trip or holiday. It's worth noting any differences between airlines if your journey involves multiple carriers and also the type of flight ticket you have purchased as the baggage allowance can vary.

The following is the general information, and before you travel, make sure you check your baggage allowance with the airline you are flying.

Each passenger can carry 1 piece of baggage with linear dimensions (the sum of height, width, and length of each baggage) not exceeding 62 inches, plus 1 piece of baggage with linear dimensions not exceeding 55 inches. One or more additional pieces, totaling no more than 45 inches may be carried on board provided it fits beneath the seat or in approved carry-on compartment.[16] Approximate dimensions are not to exceed 9×13×23. In addition to size, each piece must not exceed the weight limits. The baggage allowances vary depending on the fare.[17]

Korean Airlines has it that overweight baggage within the 2 piece free baggage allowance weighing between 23kg(50lbs) - 32kg(70lbs) will be charged at the rate of $50 USD per kilogram if departing from Korea, or will be charged at the rate of 1.5% of adult one-way normal IATA

---

16) All carry-on luggages must fit in the overhead bin or under the seat in front of you. In addition to a personal item (overcoat, laptop, purse) passengers are allowed one carry-on bag whose dimensions (length + height + width) does not exceed 115cm/45ins and which does not weigh more than 12kg/25lbs. (Korean airlines)

17) Free baggage allowances regarding size, weight, and quantity of baggage vary with passenger itinerary, seating class, and membership grade. You have to confirm the free baggage allowance that pertains to you prior to departure. e.g. To/from/via USA, US territories, Canada, First Class 2 Pieces (max. 32kg per piece) Each piece must be within 158cm in size. Prestige Class 2 Pieces (max. 32kg per piece). Each piece must be within 158cm in size. Economy Class 2 Pieces (max. 23kg per piece) Each piece may not exceed 158cm in size, and the size of the two pieces combined may not exceed 273cm. (http://www.koreanair.com/)

published fare from origin to destination per 1kg(2lbs) outside Americas. After completing check-in procedures, passengers should stand by near the counter for approximately 5 minutes until the X-ray screening of baggage has been completed. If no issue is found, passengers are then free to proceed to the boarding gate.

Vocabulary

- baggage allowance
- carrier
- approximate
- compartment

- regulations
- exceed
- overhead bin

- the type of flight ticket
- linear dimension
- carry-on luggage

Comprehension

1. What is the free baggage allowance?
   For the weight _____
   For the size _____
2. Convert 62 inch into _____ cm, and 70 pounds into _____ kg
3. How much should you pay for excess baggage?

Lets practice Metric Conversions

Pound to Kilogram

The imperial pound is officially defined as 0.453 kilograms. The kilogram is the base unit of mass in the International (SI) System of Units, and is accepted on a day-to-day basis as a unit of weight.

Inch to Centimeter

Since 1959, the inch has been defined and internationally accepted as being equivalent to 2.54cm. The centimeter is a unit of length in the metric system, equal to one-hundredth of a meter. 1cm is equivalent to 0.39370 inches.

3. Baggage Liability

As for the checked baggage, airlines have the liability[18] for loss, delay, or damage. Liability for lost, delayed, or damaged baggage will be limited as indicated below, unless a higher valuation for checked baggage has been declared and additional charges paid at check-in. Excess valuation may not be declared on certain types of articles, such as jewelry, negotiable instruments, currency and antiques. Here is the American Airline's liability limitation:

Liability for loss, delay or damage to baggage is limited to:
- Domestic travel — up to $3,500 USD per ticketed passenger
- International travel governed by the Montreal Convention — up to 1,131 SDR (Special Drawing Rights) per ticketed passenger

Baggage Liability Restrictions
- Maximum liability is not automatic — damage or loss value must be proven
- American Airlines does not assume liability for unsuitably packed items
- American Airlines does not assume liability for loss, damage or delay of baggage that may result from a security search conducted by any local, state, or federal agency

📖 Vocabulary
- liability
- declare
- unaccompanied baggage checked baggage
- valuation: the determination of the economic value of an asset
- check
- claim
- negotiable instruments: banknote, paper money

---

18) a financial obligation

🎓 Comprehension

1. Explain the liability for checked baggage.
2. Find the terms that are similar to baggage.

👥 Discussion

1. If you have any experience with overweight charge for excess baggage, please elaborate on it.
2. Suppose you lost your baggage during your travel, what should you do?

4. Restricted Carry-on Items

Any items that may be used to pose a threat to passengers in any way cannot be carried on-board. Such items include, but are not limited to, all types of knives and cutting instruments, golf clubs, clubs/bats, scissors, nail clippers, batteries, etc. If a passenger possesses any such item at the time of boarding, it must be checked at the gate.

The following items (small quantity of personal care products and/or cosmetics, lighter or matchbox, airline-approved medical items, gas-powered hair curlers, medical equipment, batteries, etc.) may be carried on board with special precautions.

Due to heightened security measures by the United States Transportation Security Administration, it is strictly prohibited to carry any form of lighters on all flights departing from/arriving in the United States (including Guam).

Car keys, pills, critical medicine or other items necessary for your health or well-being should remain in carry-on luggage whenever possible, as baggage, checked prior to departure, is generally unavailable again until claimed at your destination.

Vocabulary

- precautions
- prohibit
- security
- on-board

Comprehension

1. Why does the airline regulate the carry-on board items?
2. Which items are not allowed to carry on board?

Discussion

1. If you have any experience of being checked at the security counter, please discuss it with your partner.
2. If you want to carry tube-type cosmetics on board, what should you do?
3. If you carry the water bottle, can you pass the security counter?

6
CHAPTER

In-flight Services

1. Seats & Meals

The seat division of the airline is generally the prestige and the economy class. The prestige class can be further divided into first class seats and the business seats, and the economy class into economy seats and the coach seats.

Complimentary meals are served aloft at all meal times, both the prestige and economy class. Snack and beverage services are available aloft at all times. Wines, beer and spirits are free of charge to the prestige class

passengers and for sale to economy class passengers at reasonable prices. Passengers requiring special foods or diets are asked to make their requirements known at the time of booking in order that arrangements can be made to fulfill their requests.

Prestige classes give you spacious seating comfort and most luxurious personalized service: complimentary cocktails, gourmet dining, and a variety of other amenities.

Economy offers the same comfortable seating as prestige, with meals including coffee, tea, and soft drinks. Coach seating is comfortable but more compact and meals are hot, delicious, and satisfying. Liquors, wines, etc. are available at a normal charge in both coach and economy. All these services include the friendly hospitality of the employees.

When you check in for a long-distance flight, you will, as a general rule, be shown a diagram of the plane's interior and asked to select a seat. There are decided advantages and disadvantages to almost any location.

The first row just behind the bulkhead is the coveted spot, as it has the largest leg space. It is however, given to a passenger with an infant; the remaining first-row places are available on a first-come first-served basis.

If you have a tendency to motion sickness, avoid the rear of the aircraft and also stay away from the window seats: the seats near the wing are supposed to be stable and best in this case. Sitting near the galley, you may be among the first in the in-flight meal services, which vary according to the airlines, aircraft, and flights. Some people prefer window seats for the view and comfort; but if you are long-legged or feel caged-in, pick an aisle seat. If you feel airsickness due to rough weather, reach for the paper bag in the pocket in front of you, and buzz for the attendant. She will rush you quick soothing pills.

Even if the "SEAT BELT" sign is turned off in flight, it is recommended that you keep your seat belt fastened, whenever you are in your seat. Federal Aviation Regulations require your seat back and tray table to be upright and locked during taxi, take-off and landing. Federal Aviation Regulations require any article of baggage carried aboard to be placed under a passenger seat.

No person shall drink any alcoholic beverage aboard unless such beverage has been served to him by the air carrier operating aircraft. Alcoholic beverages cannot be served to minors.

Vocabulary

- complimentary meal
- for sale
- gourmet dining
- liquor
- bulkhead
- hospitality
- window seats
- attendant
- seat back
- upright

- aloft
- special food
- amenity
- coach
- bassinet
- motion sickness
- aisle seat
- keep your seat belt fastened
- tray table
- taxi

- free of charge
- requirement
- spirit
- economy
- first-come-first-served
- minor
- galley

Comprehension

1. What are the class divisions of seats on the plane?
2. Explain the service differences based on the class divisions.
3. If you have a tendency to motion sickness, which seat is best for you?
4. If you are long-legged, which seat is good for you?
5. According to Federal Aviation Regulations, you have to fasten your seat belt at least in these situations such as _____.

Discussion

1. Give some examples of alcoholic beverages.
2. Explain the difference between spirit and liquor.
3. Who is a minor? Are you legally allowed to drink alcoholic beverages?

2. Unaccompanied Minors (UM) Service

Children under the age of 5, under no circumstance, can travel alone. Children the age of 5-12 are eligible to Unaccompanied Minors (UM) service. You should contact the reservation center at least 24 hours prior to departure time and receive confirmation of your application, and provide details of the adults (name, relationship, address and telephone number), who are to accompany the child to the departure point and meet the child at the destination. No Service Fees are required.[19] (Domestic flights: Child fare applied, International flights: Adult fare applied.)

Vocabulary

- eligible
- confirmation
- accompany

Comprehension

1. Explain UM service in English.
2. If you want to request UM service, you should apply it prior to _____ at the latest.

---

[19] Adolescents between the age of 12 to 16 can apply for the Unaccompanied Minors (UM) service for international flights, if they travel with Korean Air only. Service fee (USD 60) must be paid.

3. Special Meals Request

Airlines offer special meals to meet specific dietary requirements for health or religious reasons. A special meal can be requested at the time of booking or by adding a request to an existing reservation. Special Meals must be ordered at least 24 hours prior to departure. The following is the examples:

Vegetarian Meals

Neither meat, poultry, fish of any kinds nor product with lard and gelatin are used. Yet meals can contain egg and dairy products are allowed. Main ingredients are grains, fruit, vegetables and vegetable oil.

Medical Meals

For passengers with special dietary requirements due to medical reasons, airlines offer a wide range of medical meals which are carefully prepared and produced, based on medical and nutritional expertise, e.g. Low Fat Meal, Diabetic Meal, Low Calorie Meal, Low Salt Meal, etc.

Religious Meals

Moslem Meal is prepared according to Halal rules (No Pork & alcohol). Hindu Meal is prepared for Hindus (No Beef & Veal). Kosher Meal is prepared for Jews according to Jewish dietary laws.

Child Meals

In addition to these, Infant Meal and Child Meal are provided. This meal is available for children ages 2-12, and includes food offerings that appeal to children. The meals planned follow Recommended Dietary Allowances for children.

Vocabulary

- poultry
- ingredient
- dairy products
- dietary

- nutritional   • expertise: skill, knowledge, know-how

Comprehension

1. Some people need special foods. Think of the reasons and provide some examples.

7

Foreign Currency

A currency refers to money in any form in actual use or circulation as a medium of exchange. In the first stage of currency, metals were used as symbols to represent value stored in the form of commodities, e.g. first silver, then both silver and gold, and at one point also bronze and copper. In pre-modern China, the need for credit and for a medium of exchange that was less physically cumbersome than large numbers of copper coins led to the introduction of paper money, i.e. banknotes. It reduced the need to transport gold and silver, which was risky. By 1900, most of the industrializing nations were on some form of gold standard, with paper notes and silver coins constituting the circulating medium.

Here are the examples of currencies: United States Dollar: USD ($), European Union Euro: EUR (€), Japanese yen: JPY (¥), United Kingdom Pound sterling: GBP (£),[20] Chinese yuan: CNY (¥), Korean won: KRW

---

20) Everyone is familiar with the currency of the United Kingdom which is more commonly known as the pound. Sometimes, however, the word "sterling" is used to describe the UK currency. For formal contexts, the full, official name is used which is *poundsterling*. The pound sterling, generally shortened to just "pound," is the certified currency of the United Kingdom. The United Kingdom currency is more known by the word "pound" while "sterling" is used in the financial market. The pound sterling is the oldest currency being used in the world. Both are used all over

(□). Those four currencies at the front are the most-traded currencies in the world's foreign exchange market, and make up the basket of currencies for the calculation of the value of the IMF Special Drawing Rights (partly excerpted from en.wikipedia.org).

The basic units of American money are dollars (symbolized as $) and cents (symbolized as C).[21] When carrying American money, you have small-denomination bills.[22] It is also useful to make a habit of carrying coins for phone calls, and vending-machines. There are no limitations on the amount of American or foreign money you may bring into the United States. In the 20th Century, the best way to bring money into the country was in the form of travelers checks issued in dollar amounts, but the trend is changing to the form of cards.

Vocabulary

- circulation
- cumbersome
- denomination
- vending machine

- medium: a way or means
- constitute
- small denomination bill
- sterling:

- commodity
- currency

Comprehension

1. Early in history, what was used for currency?
2. Which country first introduced the paper money?
3. Which currencies are the most traded in the world?
4. What are the basic units of American money?
5. What kinds of denomination bills are used for the distinction of value in

the world and only differ depending on the circumstance. http://www.differencebetween.net/business/finance-business-2/difference-between-pound-and-sterling/

21) All dollar bills are green: no color distinction is made for the different denominations. Pennies are copper alloy, and all other coins are silver-colored alloy. The commonly used names of the coins are: 1 ¢ = penny, 5 ¢ = nickel, 10 ¢ = dime, 25 ¢ = quarter.

22) For some small shops will not accept anything larger than a $20 bill in payment for a minor purchase.

American money?

6. Which denomination bill is the most widely used in America?

👥 Discussion

1. What is the difference between the pound and the sterling?
2. Illustrate the symbols of each currency presented in the above article.

1. Traveler's Checks

Traveler's checks were first issued in 1772 by the London Credit Exchange Company for use in ninety European cities, and in 1874, Thomas Cook was issuing 'circular notes' that operated in the manner of traveler's checks.

American Express was the first company to develop a large-scale traveler's check system in 1891, and is still the largest issuer of traveler's checks today by volume. Between the 1950s and the 1990s, traveler's checks became one of the main ways that people took money on vacation for use in foreign countries without the risks associated with carrying large amounts of cash.

Traveler's checks are sold by banks and financial specialist to customers for use at a later time.[23] Upon obtaining custody of a purchased supply of traveler's checks, the purchaser should immediately write his or her signature once upon each, usually on the check's upper portion.[24] This helps protect them if they are stolen. The purchaser will also have received a receipt and some other documentation that should be kept in a safe place other than where he or she carries the checks. Traveler's checks can usually be replaced if lost or stolen (if the owner still has the receipt issued with the purchase of the checks showing the serial numbers allocated).

The use has been in decline since the 1990s as alternatives, such as credit cards, debit cards, and automated teller machines became more widely available and were easier and more convenient for travelers. In 2005, American Express released the American Express Travelers Check Card, a stored-value card that serves the same purposes as a traveler's check, but can be used in stores like a credit card. It discontinued the card in October 2007. A number of other financial companies went on to issue stored-value or pre-paid debit cards containing several currencies that could be used like credit or debit cards at shops and at ATMs, mimicking the

---

23) 1% commission is charged for the purchase of traveler's checks.

24) When spending it, you must countersign it before the recipient. It was accepted as readily as native currency nearly anywhere.

traveler's check in electronic form. One of the major examples is the Visa Travel Money card.

Vocabulary

- issuer
- signature
- decline
- allocated
- specialist

- financial
- receipt
- alternative
- discontinued
- purchaser

- custody
- documentation
- receipt
- release

- automated teller machines (ATM): an electronic telecommunications device that enables the customers of a financial institution to perform financial transactions without the need for a human cashier, clerk or bank teller.
- serial numbers: a unique code assigned for identification of a single unit debit cards: a plastic payment card with which a payment is made, while most relay a message to the cardholder's bank to withdraw funds from a payer's designated bank account

Comprehension

1. Which company first issued the traveler's check in large volumes?
2. Explain the way to use a traveler's check.
3. What was the best way to bring money into a foreign country between 1950s and 1990s? And why?
4. How much is charged to purchase a traveler's check?
5. Why did the use of traveler's check decline?
6. What are the alternatives to the traveler's check? Give some examples.

Discussion

1. Explain hard currency.
2. Find nicknames of the American dollar note.
   e.g. a dollar bill = buck, greenback, green

2. Exchange and Re-exchange

The price of currency fluctuates just like that of any other commodity. An exchange rate is the price at which two currencies can be exchanged against each other. This is used for trade between the two currency zones. A currency pair is the quotation of the relative value of a currency unit against the unit of another currency in the foreign exchange market. The quotation EUR/USD 1.3533 means that 1 Euro is able to buy 1.3533 US dollar. In other words, this is the price of a unit of Euro in US dollar. Here, EUR is called the "Fixed currency", while USD is called the "Variable currency" (partly excerpted from en.wikipedia.org).

European currencies, however, are so stable that they fluctuate hardly at all. For the exchange of foreign currency for local currency, banks at airports, air terminals, or main train stations, are often available even in the late or early hours.

Avoid leaving any foreign country with a sizable chunk of its currency. Surplus bills can normally be passed in the next country, but leftover foreign change is not usable: try to get rid of all coins (except souvenirs) before crossing the border.

Vocabulary

- fluctuate
- variable
- transaction
- rates of exchange
- surplus bills
- balance
- quotation
- souvenir

Comprehension

1. What is exchange rate?
2. Explain the quotation EUR/USD 1.3533.
3. Where can you exchange foreign currency?

👥 Discussion

1. Discuss the exchange rates of Won to other foreign currencies.
2. If you win the 100 million dollar lottery, which country would you like to go with it?

8

Duty-free Shopping

Duty-free shops (or stores) are retail outlets that are exempt from the payment of certain local or national taxes and duties, on the requirement that the goods sold will be sold to travelers who will take them out of the country. Duty-free shops are often found in the international zone of international airports, sea ports, and train stations but goods  can be also bought duty-free on board airplanes and passenger ships.

The world's first duty-free shop was established at Shannon Airport, Ireland in 1947. The Irish Parliament ruled that any goods brought directly into Shannon Airport from abroad would not be liable to duty or local taxes.[25] It was a historic decision that paved the way for the phenomenal growth of duty-free shopping throughout the world.

Several locales grew as duty-free shopping destinations. They are exem-

---

25) Designed to provide a service for Trans-Atlantic airline passengers typically travelling between Europe and North America whose flights stopped for refueling on both outbound and inbound legs of their journeys, it was an immediate success.

plified by Saint Martin and the U.S. Virgin Islands in the Caribbean, Hong Kong and Singapore. Still others claim prices competitive to duty-free. Generally, goods are free of duty and tax levied on imports for sale anywhere in the shopping destination. Merchants may pay inventory/ business or other taxes, but their customers usually pay none directly.

The duty-free goods mean goods sold at prices lower than their equivalent in the normal market at home.[26] Some of the popular duty-free items are liquor, cigarettes, cigars, perfumes, cameras, watches, radios, and many other articles for daily use. When you buy them at airport shops, you may be asked to show your ticket or boarding card to prove you are a departing or transit passenger. Moreover, in many cases, your purchases must remain in bond until you leave the area. In other words, you are given a receipt for your purchase but not the items, which are put either into the "in bond" window at the airport (where you collect them), or directly aboard your plane. You may also have a chance for a duty-free purchase during an international flight, though the items sold are limited in variety and quantity.

Most tax regimes also allow travelers entering a country to bring in a certain amount of goods for personal use without paying tax on them, the so-called "duty-free allowance"; because it is not economically justifiable to collect the small amounts of tax involved, and would be an inconvenience to the passengers.

Vocabulary

• duty	• local tax	• retail
• outlets	• exemplify	• levy
• competitive	• exemption	• elimination
• middlemen	• profits	• duty-free items
• article	• boarding card	• transit passenger
• departing passenger	• in bond window	

---

26) The reason why they cost less is a result not only of the exemption of duty but of local taxes and of elimination of profits made by several middlemen in importing.

🎓 Comprehension

1. What is the origin of duty-free shopping?
2. What are the reasons that the prices of duty-free goods are lower than that of their equivalents?
3. Give some examples of duty-free items. ﹀
4. Where can you buy duty-free goods?
5. When you purchase duty-free goods, you have to show _____ and

   _____ .
6. Explain the difference between cigarettes and cigars.
   Take similar examples. e.g. banquette
7. Give some examples of duty-free shopping destinations.
8. Explain the duty-free allowance.

👥 Discussion

1. When you're traveling, do you often use duty-free shops?
2. Which item do you usually purchase, and why?
3. When you purchase duty-free goods, there is a purchase limitation by law. What is the limit to purchase?

PART III

Tourist Industry

Tourist Industry

The travel and tourism industry is one of the world's largest industries with a global economic contribution (direct, indirect and induced) of over 7.6 trillion U.S. dollars in 2016. The direct economic impact of the industry, including accommodation, transportation, entertainment and attractions, was approximately 2.3 trillion U.S. dollars that year. Europe receives the most international tourist arrivals, and produces the most travelers: with approximately 607 million outbound tourists in 2015 (partly excepted from www.statista.com.).

1. Kinds of Tourists

Worldwide, the tourism industry has experienced steady growth almost every year. Indeed, the growth rate of tourism has generally exceeded the growth rate for the worldwide economy. Sometimes it seems as though a new *resort* area springs up every day wherever there are sun and sea.[1]

---

1) The shores of the Mediterranean and Caribbean Seas and the Pacific coastlines of Mexico,

In spite of this rapid growth, it is not easy to define tourism, and accurate statistics are not easy to obtain.[2] Considering the purpose of travel, there are two divisions of tourists; **recreational travelers and business travelers**.

Tourism necessarily involves travel. People travel for the purpose of recreation or pleasure; they are people on holiday.[3] Other people travel for reasons of health. Some others travel to visit friends or relatives, because of increased mobility throughout the world. Still others travel in order to educate themselves in accord with the old precept that travel is broadening. These people are generally considered as recreational tourists since the primary reason for their trips is personal.

Another group of people is those who are traveling on business. Among them are businessmen and government officials as well as people attending meetings or conventions. Other type of business travel is the incentive trip.[4] People traveling on business often combine pleasure with their work.

These two groups of tourists have different marketing approaches. The recreational travelers respond to lower fares and other inducements in pricing, in selecting the destination. They make up **a price elastic market**, whereas the business groups, on the other hand, make up **a price inelastic market**.[5] Business travelers also make more trips to large cities or industrial centers than to resort areas. It should be noted that some large cities, such as London, Paris, New York, Rome, and Tokyo, are themselves the most important tourist destinations in the world.

Florida, and Hawaii are only a few of the areas that have been intensively developed in the past few years.

2) Not included in the area of tourism are people who travel someplace in order to take up a job. This excludes from tourism the migrants; Students who study abroad in a regular school are also not included in tourist statistics.

3) Originally, both the Riviera and Switzerland were *tourist destinations* as health resorts.

4) A bonus or reward is given, for example, to a salesman who has exceeded his quota.

5) Their trips are not scheduled according to lower fares, the destination is determined in advance, and the expense is usually paid for by their employers. They are looking for dependable rather than inexpensive service.

Vocabulary

- resort
- mobility
- Inducements
- incentive
- tourist
- precept
- combine
- price elastic market
- excursionist
- conventions
- tourist destination
- price inelastic market

Comprehension

1. Provide some examples of the resort areas.
2. What are the two major classifications of tourists?
3. What specific purposes do recreational tourists have in mind?
4. Provide some examples of business travelers.
5. For marketing purposes, recreational travelers and business travelers should be approached differently. Explain the difference in English.
6. Which travelers are usually not included in tourist statistics?

2. Tourism and Transportation

Tourism is a relatively new phenomenon in the world. Tourism as we know it today began with the building of the railroads in the 19th Century.[6] In fact, the words **tourism** and **tourist** themselves were not used until about 1800. Since 1841 when the first tour in the modern sense was put together by Thomas Cook in England, the firm of Thomas Cook and Sons has remained one of the prominent names in the tourist industry.

Steamships also increased tourism, especially across the North Atlantic, the major route of modern tourism. The automobile and the airplane in still more recent times have also become major modes of transportation for recreational purposes. The greatest growth in international tourism has taken place only since the end of World War II in 1945, and it has paralleled the growth of air transportation.

Culpan (1987) identified transportation modes and management as the "important ingredients of the international tourism system," providing the linkage by air, sea and land modes for tourists as well as the availability of support services. The improvement in transportation modes and the resonable fares have increased the accessibility of areas once considered off-the-beaten-path. In spite of the fact that the advent of flight has shrunk the world, and the motor vehicle has made travel to anywhere possible, accesses to tourist sites vary according to the nature of the site, the state of infrastructure, and the efficiency of the public transport system.

Tourists are the persons who wish to travel with spare time and money (Timur and Olali, 1988:45), and the efficient transportation modes provide the tourists with disposable time and energy enough to see as many places as possible and enjoy the travel. Thus it is largely due to the improvement of transportation that tourism has expanded (partly excepted from Mammadov 2012).

---

6) Since being away from home is a necessary component of tourism, its development as a mass industry depended on modern means of rapid and inexpensive transportation.

Vocabulary

- Phenomenon
- off-the-beaten-path
- prominent
- linkage
- parallel
- accessibility

Comprehension

1. The development of tourism as a mass industry is dependent on _____.
2. When was the words "tourist" and "tourism" first used?
3. When and by whom was the first tour in the modern sense put together?
4. Give some examples of transportation that played an important role in tourism.

3. Tourism and Industrialization

Industrialization has produced the other conditions that are necessary for tourism. Among them is the creation of middle class with an amount of **disposable income**.[7] Another important condition is urbanization, the growth of large cities.[8]

With industrialization, the concept of leisure in the form of long weekends and **paid vacations**[9] has spread to the working class, and this may be the most important factor in modern tourism.

Sun-and-sea areas that are near the major markets for tourists derive a large part of their income from tourism.[10] One of the principal reasons for encouraging a tourist industry in many developing countries is the so-called **multiplier effect**[11] of the tourist dollar. In some countries the multiplier can be a factor as high as 3, but it is often a lower number because of **leakage**.[12] Another attraction of the tourist industry for the developing countries is that it is **labor-intensive**.[13] This is a common feature of service industries, which deal with intangible products - like a holiday rather than tangible products - like an electric toaster.

---

7) Income above and beyond what is needed for basic expenses such as food, shelter, clothing, and taxes.

8) Residents of the big population centers take more holiday trips than residents of rural areas. Anyone who has been to Paris in August, for example, cannot help but observe that a great many of the inhabitants—with the exception of those who serve foreign tourists—are away on vacation.

9) This subsidized recreational travel is also called *social tourism,* for residents of Russia and the other Communist countries.

10) On the Mediterranean, Spain, Portugal, Greece, Morocco, and Tunisia as well as off the coast of the United States, the Bahamas and Bermuda among others attract large numbers of tourists. It has been estimated that in the Bahamas an income of more than $1,500 a year per person can be attributed to tourism.

11) Money paid for wages or in other ways is spent not once but sometimes several times for other items in the economy—the food that hotel employees eat at home, for example, or the houses in which they live, or the durable goods that they buy.

12) Leakage comes from the money that goes out of the economy either in the form of imports that are necessary to sustain the tourist industry or in profits that are drained off by investors. In some tourist areas, it has been necessary to import workers. The U.S. Virgin Islands is one example. However, many of these workers cause leakages in the form of remittances to their home countries.

13) It requires a large number of workers in proportion to the people who are served.

🅐 Vocabulary

- disposable income
- social tourism
- labor intensive

- urbanization
- multiplier effect
- intangible

- paid vacation
- leakage

🎓 Comprehension

1. Explain how industrialization has an important influence on tourism.
2. Give some examples of the paid vacation.
3. What is disposable income?
4. What is the multiplier effect?
5. How does leakage reduce the multiplier effect? Give some examples of leakages?
6. What makes the tourist industry attractive in the developing countries?

👥 Discussion

The multiplier effect refers to the increase in final income arising from any new injection of spending. The extent of the multiplier effect in increasing domestic business activity is dependent upon the marginal propensity to consume (mpc), and marginal propensity to save (mps). When income is spent, this spending becomes someone else's income, and so on. Marginal propensities show the proportion of extra income allocated to particular activities, such as investment spending by firms, saving by households, and spending on imports from abroad. The following general formula to calculate the multiplier uses marginal propensities, as follows: 1/1-mpc

Question: Suppose that 80% of all new income in a given period of time is spent on the products, calculate the multiplier effect.

Answer: The marginal propensity to consume would be 80/100, which is 0.8. Hence, if consumers spend 0.8 and save 0.2 of every dollar of extra income, the multiplier will be: $1/1 - 0.8 = 1/0.2 = 5$

The fact that the multiplier is 5, means that every dollar of new income generates 5 dollars of extra income. (http://www.economic-sonline.co.uk/Managing_the_economy/The_multiplier_effect.html)

2

Tourism and Transportation

1. Kinds of Transportation

Being in a different place from one's usual residence is an essential feature of tourism.[14] This means that transportation companies are one vital aspect in the total tourist industry. Without modern high-speed forms of transportation, tourism would be possible only for a tiny fraction of the population. Transportation links the various destinations. It is largely due to the improvement of transportation that tourism has expanded. The advent of flight has shrunk the world, and the motor vehicle has made travel to anywhere possible.

During the 19th Century, railroads spread and formed the first successful system of mass transportation. Thomas Cook as a frontrunner of establishing tourism system conducted the first organized tour in 1841, which conveyed about 500 passengers in open carriages from Leicester to

---

14) The expansion of international tourism has a large impact on the discipline of transport geography. As of 2010, 877 million international tourist receipts were accounted for, representing more than 10% of the global population.

Loughborough, the enormous distance of 12 miles for a shilling per person, and thus made Mass Tourism possible. Steamships were developed about the same time as railroads, and by 1900, they were carrying passengers and freight on all the oceans of the world.

Rail travel was the dominant form of mass public transport before the age of the automobile. Even if trains are very fast, the network is not too flexible, pre-established routes have to be followed. The railway network usually reflects more the commercial needs of the national economy than the holiday tourist flow, which can make it a second choice as a traveling mode. Unfortunately for those people who prefer leisurely travel, both railroads[15] and steamships have lost much of their business and replaced by automobiles.[16]

Automobile traveling is usually an independent means of transport. The driver decides where, when and how he is going to get to a destination. It is usually cheaper since roads fees are not directly paid but rather from taxes. It is the only transportation mode that does not require transfers, in the sense that the whole journey, from door to door, can be achieve without even stopping. Car transport is the dominant mode in world tourism (77% of all journeys), notably because of advantages such as flexibility, price, and independence.

As for the sea transportation, regularly scheduled steamship passenger service has almost disappeared, but ships still play an important part in tourism: A **cruise** is a voyage by ship, and the cruise ship acts as the hotel for the passengers as well as their means of transportation.[17] Cruises are mainly concentrated towards short sea journeys of about a week. Cruising has become a significant tourist industry; big cruisers are like floating resorts where guests can enjoy luxury and entertainment while moving towards their multiple destinations. The international market for cruising

---

15) In the United States, the only remaining route that offers adequate passenger service is between New York and Washington.

16) The automobile offers convenience. The traveler can depart from his own home and arrive at his destination without transferring baggage or having to cope with any of the other difficulties that would ordinarily confront him.

17) When the tourists reach a port, they are usually conducted on one-day excursions, but return to the ship to eat and to sleep. A majority of cruise ships operate in the "warm seas," the Caribbean and the Mediterranean. Smaller and lighter ships that are especially designed for cruising have been built in recent years.

was about 18.3 million tourists in 2010, which involves an annual growth rate above 7% since 1990. The main cruise markets are the Caribbean and the Mediterranean, and Alaska and Northern Europe fjords are also popular during the summer season.

For a long-distance travel, the airplane has replaced the railroad and the ship. **Air transport** is by far the most effective transport mode. Notably because of prices, only 12.5% of the tourist travel by plane, but for international travel this share is around 40%. Air transport has revolutionized the geographical aspect of distances; the most remote areas can now be attained, any journey around the world can be measured in terms of hours of traveling. Business people are among the biggest users of airline facilities, but low cost air carriers have attracted a significant market segment.[18]

The airlines have two kinds of operations, scheduled and nonscheduled. A **scheduled airline** operates on fixed routes at fixed times according to a timetable, which is available to the public. A **nonscheduled airline** operates on routes and at times when there is a demand for the service,[19] in other words, a charter operation. The **load factor** is the percentage of seats that have been sold on a flight.[20]

Vocabulary

• dominant	• pre-established routes	• transport
• transfer	• flexibility	• voyage
• annual growth rate	• revolutionize	• Caribbean
• Mediterranean	• low cost air carriers	• fjords
• cruise	• car ferry	• car rental agency
• scheduled airline	• charter plane	• load factor

---

18) Excerpt from Jean-Paul Rodrigue (2013) *The Geography of Transport System.*

19) The nonscheduled airlines got a start largely as a result of government business e.g. International crises like the Berlin Airlift and the Vietnamese War

20) A scheduled flight needed a load factor of a little over 50 percent at regular fares to assure a profit.

🎓 Comprehension

1. Transportation is a vital aspect of the total tourist industry. Explain the reasons.
2. When was the first railroad built? And what was the effect on tourism?
3. In what way does the automobile offer convenience?
4. What has become a principal mode of transportation for long-distance travel?
5. Take some examples of car rental agency.
6. The percentage of seats sold on an airplane is _____.
7. What was a profitable percentage for the airplane?

👥 Discussion

1. When you travel, which mode of transportation do you mostly use? And Why?
2. Think about the advantages and disadvantages of couch travels, train travels, and automobile travels.
3. If you have any experience traveling in Europe by the train pass, please share it with the class.

2. Travel Package & Airline

A package tour or package holiday consists of transport and accommodation advertised and sold together by a vendor known as a tour operator. Transport can be via charter airline to a foreign country, and may also include travel between areas as part of the holiday. Package holidays are organized by a tour operator and sold to a consumer by a travel agent. Some travel agents are employees of tour operators, others are independent.

In the United Kingdom, the cheap package holidays — which combined flight, transfers, and accommodation — provided the first chance for most people to have affordable travel abroad by the late 1950s and 1960s. Despite opening up mass tourism, the package tour industry declined during the 1970s, and the trend for package holiday bookings revived in 2009, with a greater financial security in the holiday and flight companies,[21] and 'no-frills' flights increased. Coupled with the search for late holidays as holiday makers left booking to the last moment, this led to a rise in consumers booking package holidays.[22]

As seating capacity increased with the introduction of newer, larger, and faster planes, the airlines were able to offer a percentage of their seats for sale through travel agents or tour operators. By means of these special fares, they were able to increase their business. **IT** stands for inclusive tour, a travel package that offers both transportation and accommodations, and often entertainment as well. **ITX** stands for tour-basing fares. They are offered by scheduled airlines to travel agents or tour operators who sell the package to the general public. Another is **CIT**, charter inclusive tour, one that utilizes a charter airplane for transportation.

The nonscheduled airlines chartered entire flights to groups that were traveling to the same destination, e.g. members of a music society attending the Salzburg Festival. Groups traveling to the same place for a similar purpose are called **affinity** groups.

All transportation is subject to regulation by government, but the airlines

---

21) In the UK, the downturn in the package holiday market led to the consolidation of the tour operator market (The major operators are Thomson Holidays and First Choice part of TUI AG and Thomas Cook AG.).

22) Excerpted from wikipedia.

are among the most completely regulated of all carriers.[23] Fares on international services are set by agreement through IATA, the International Air Transport Association.[24]

 Vocabulary

- inclusive tours   • IT   • CIT   • affinity group

Comprehension

1. What are some of the important abbreviations connected with packaged tours?
2. What is the difference between IT and CIT?
3. What is the term for a group traveling to the same place for a similar purpose called? Give some examples.
4. A nonscheduled airline is similar to _____.

---

23) The routes they can fly, the number of flights, and many other matters are controlled by means of bilateral agreements between different countries in the case of international airlines, e.g. CAB in the U.S.A..

24) IATA with headquarters at Montreal is a voluntary association of the airlines, but almost all the international scheduled carriers are members.

3. Rail Transport

Rail transport is a means of con- veyance of passengers and goods, by way of wheeled vehicles running on rails. A passenger train travels bet- ween stations where passengers may embark and disembark. The oversight of the train is the duty of a guard/ train manager/conductor. Passenger

trains are part of public transport and often make up the stem of the service, with buses feeding to stations. Passenger trains provide long-distance intercity travel, daily commuter trips, or local urban transit services. They even include a diversity of vehicles, operating speeds, right-of-way requirements, and service frequency. Passenger trains usually can be divided into two operations: intercity railway and intracity transit. Whereas as intercity railway involve higher speeds, longer routes, and lower frequency (usually scheduled), intracity transit involves lower speeds, shorter routes, and higher frequency (especially during peak hours).

Intercity trains are long-haul trains that operate with few stops between cities. Trains typically have amenities such as a dining car. Some lines also provide over-night services with sleeping cars. Some long-haul trains have been given a specific name. Regional trains are medium distance trains that connect cities with outlying, surrounding areas, or provide a regional service, making more stops and having lower speeds. Commuter trains serve suburbs of urban areas, providing a daily commuting service. Airport rail links provide quick access from city centers to airports.

High-speed rails are special inter-city trains that operate at much higher speeds than conventional railways, the limit being regarded at 200 to 320 kilometers per hour (120 to 200 mph). High-speed trains are used mostly for long-haul service and most systems are in Western Europe and East Asia. The speed record is 574.8 km/h (357.2 mph), set by a modified French TGV.

The **sleepingcar** or **sleeper** (often *wagon-lit*) is a railway/railroad passenger car that can accommodate all its passengers in beds of one kind or another, primarily for the purpose of making nighttime travel more restful. A sleeping car is, in essence, a moving house of lodging. A night in transit can replace a hotel stay at the destination. Despite its recent overall decline in popularity, the overnight train still offers an enjoyable means of transportation for many.

In modern Europe, a substantial number of sleeping car services continue to operate, though they face strong competition from high-speed day trains and budget airlines. In some cases, trains are split and recombined in the dead of night, making it possible to offer several connections with a relatively small number of trains. Generally, the trains consist of sleeping cars with private compartments, couchette cars, and sometimes cars with normal seating.

An example of a more basic type of sleeping car is the European couchette car, which is divided into compartments for four or six people, with bench-configuration seating during the day and "privacyless" double- or triple-level bunk-beds at night. (partly excepted from en.wikipedia.org)

Vocabulary

- conveyance
- embark
- intracity transit
- compartment
- couchette
- oversight (supervision, direct)
- disembark
- long-haul trains
- corridor
- diner
- intercity railway
- commuter trains
- sleeper
- vendor

Comprehension

1. Explain seat arrangement of European trains.
2. Explain sleeping accommodations in railroads.

Eurailpass

Eurail passes[25] (formerly known as Europass) provide a passenger with unlimited ability to travel on nearly all European railroads.[26] Eurail sells a variety of passes, including those specific to two to five bordering countries, discounted passes for groups of up to five people travelling together, or for those under 26 passes which provide unlimited travel in a fixed period, and passes which provide a fixed number of days of travel. Rail Passes become a great benefit if you plan to take many trains, not just a couple of smaller train trips.

Student rail passes

A Eurailpass generally grants a passenger free transportation on an ordinary train, e.g. EuroCity trains and Regional.[27] The Student Railpass is for unlimited second-class train travel in a cost effective way. Both Eurailpass and Eurail Youthpass can only be purchased by non-European residents: you have to purchase before leaving for Europe.[28] A passport is required for issuing the rail pass, and the buyer of the Eurail Youthpass should prove to be a full-time student between the age of 14 and 26. The validity of the Eurailpass begins the first day the holder actually uses it for a trip; the Eurailpass must be validated at the ticket office of the station at his first departure, when the clerk writes on the pass both the first and last day it can be used.

Both passes are non-replaceable and non-refundable if either lost or

---

25) The Eurorail (Informally known as Eurail) Group G.I.E. is a Netherlands-based company, registered in Luxembourg, that sells passes and tickets for European railroads to residents of Europe and other countries. It is owned by a group of European rail carriers and shipping companies.

26) The traditional Eurail pass covers 28 countries, as of 2013: Austria, Belgium, Bulgaria, Croatia, Czech Republic, Denmark, Finland, France, Germany, Greece, Hungary, Ireland, Italy, Luxembourg, Montenegro, Netherlands, Northern Ireland, Norway, Poland, Portugal, Romania, Serbia, Slovakia, Slovenia, Spain, Sweden, Switzerland, and Turkey.

27) Trains that require reservations are referred to as premier trains, these trains include; TGV, Thalys, Eurostar, Eurostar Italia, AVE, Swiss Scenic Trains and night trains (with sleeping compartments) require a supplement.

28) It is possible for non-Europeans to obtain passes in Europe, although they are cheaper and easier to procure outside of Europe. For European residents InterRail is available, which has similar benefits, except that it is not valid in the buyer's country of residence.

stolen after the first day they become valid. They are refundable at 90% of the price prior to becoming valid if they are turned in.

Vocabulary

- flat fare
- arbitrarily
- validity
- non-refundable

Comprehension

1. What are the differences between regular Eurail pass and Student railpass?
2. How does the validity begin?
3. What is the restriction to purchase the Eurail pass?
4. Name some countries and trains included in the Eurailpass.

Supplemental Information of Transportation

📖 Vocabulary

- multi-station city
- originate
- conductor
- double decker
- a time charge/ a mileage charge
- hourly/ daily/ weekly rate
- track
- designate
- underground
- odometer
- terminate
- discard
- uptown/downtown
- insurance
- liability

🎓 Comprehension

1. Explain the way to board the train in the multi-station city.
2. Explain the difference between 24:00 and 0:00.
3. What is Amtrak?
4. What is Metroliner?
5. What is Ameripass?
6. Explain the subway system in England.
7. What is "request stops"?
8. Charges for rental cars vary with _____ and _____.

👥 Discussion

1. Could you draw a subway symbol in Korea? Open the subway map and take an imaginary walk from Kyung Hee University to a certain place that your group chooses.
2. If you have any experience renting a car, please share it with the class.

3

Tour Operators

Tour operators can be considered the wholesalers of the tourist industry. Their product is the packaged tour. A tour operator typically combines tour and travel components to create a holiday. They prepare itinerary. The most common example of a tour operator's product would be a flight on a charter airline plus a transfer from the airport to a hotel and the services of a local representative, all for one price.

There are two principal kinds of packaged tours, the inclusive tour (IT), usually on the scheduled airlines, and the charter inclusive tour (CIT), usually on chartered, nonscheduled airlines. Packaged tours offer transportation, hotel accommodations, and **transfer** to and from the airport. In addition to the basic features, the tour package may also offer meals, entertainment, sightseeing, a rental car, and many other extras.

The first tour in the modern sense was put together by Thomas Cook in 1841. The firm of Thomas Cook and Sons has remained a major force in the travel industry. Its principal rival for many years has been the American Express Company.[29] Both Cook and American Express operate as tour

---

29) American Express Company, which grew out of the Wells Fargo freight forwarding business in the frontier days of the American West. American Express is the first company to issue

packagers as well as **retail travel agents**.[30] The tour operators needs a sounder financial base and they have a tendency to be absorbed by conglomerates, the modern corporations that engage in many different kinds of business. Travel agents then work directly with the tour operator to perfect client's requests. They hold the role of selling and administering packages from various tour operators to their personal clients based on what they're looking for and what package suits each client best.

It is possible to distinguish between two types of tours; one is the holiday package[31] that has a resort hotel as its destination; the second is the guided tour that features sightseeing or some other special attraction. The person who leads such tours is the tour guide.[32]

The public derives many advantages from packaged tours, the most obvious being the price. A second advantage is the opportunity for the tourist to make all his travel arrangements in one place at one time. A third advantage can be summed up in the term accessibility.[33]

The major tour operator associations are the National Tour Association (NTA) in the U.S.A, European Tour Operators Association (ETOA) in Europe, and the Association of British Travel Agents (ABTA) in the UK.

Vocabulary

- tour operator
- traveler's check
- no frill variety
- transfer
- typical package
- psychologist
- retail travel agents
- conglomerates
- guided tour

---

traveler's checks; it owns one of the major credit card services; and it also engages in international banking and insurance.

30) They sell the tours directly to the public through their own travel offices and through other agents.

31) While local sightseeing or entertainment may be included in the package, the major attractions usually include sun, sea, and activities such as golf or tennis that are offered by the resort itself.

32) The tour guide is multilingual, and relates well to other people. Dealing with the variety of problems, he/she is as much of a psychologist as a travel expert.

33) Tours, for example, now regularly go to archeological sites in the jungles of Central America— Tikal in Guatemala or Copan in Honduras. A few years ago only dedicated scientists would have undertaken the hardships of such a trip, but governments, local airlines, and tour operators have made these and countless other places throughout the world accessible to the general public.

- multi-lingual
- accessibility
- independent traveler
- archeological sites
- price inducement

🎓 Comprehension

1. What are some examples of tour operators in Korea?
2. What kinds of travel packages do tour operators put together?
3. Which features do these packages offer?
4. What is the rival company of Thomas Cook and Sons in the U.S.A.?
5. Major tour operators have an alliance with the airlines. What is the reason?
6. Why did tour operators need to find a sounder financial base?
7. What is the tour guide's job?
8. What are the advantages of the packaged tour?

👥 Discussion

1. If you have worked in the restaurant, what position would it be?
2. Do you agree that jobs in the restaurant and the hotel are semiskilled?
3. If you have experience going on a guided tour, share the experience.

PART IV

Hospitality Industry

Hotel and other food service industries are part of the Hospitality Industry. The word "Hotel" is derived from the Latin word "hospitum" i.e. the halls in olden days where guests were given hospitality, or the notion of hospitality can be described as an act of receiving and treating strangers and guest in warm, friendly and generous way without any consideration for the reward and / or return. Hospitality in the modern sense comprises of four characteristic features: (1) It is conferred by a host on a guest "a home away from home". (2) It is interactive i.e. involving the coming together of a provider and a receiver. (3) It comprises of a blend of tangible and intangible factors. (4) The host provides the guest's a sense of security and psychological and physiological comfort. The four attributes, if put into practice, deliver the desired feeling of being "at home". (partly excerpted from en.wikipedia.org)

1

Accommodations

The industry came into being in the 6th century B.C. The earliest forms of hotels were just large halls where travelers slept on the floor along with the animals on which they traveled and in the west they were known as "Inns".[1] Then changes in the mode of lodging had come with the development of vehicles, i.e. with the invention of wheels, speed of travel increased. The industrial revolution in England and other countries marked a major turning point; travel for business gradually frequented and with the growth of economy travel for recreation increased; and the meaningful

---

[1] The early travelers all belonged to particular segment of the society i.e. either they were the kings and nobles, the religious messengers, missionaries, traders and soldiers. The first class of people i.e. the kings and nobles traveled on horseback or carriages and were usually entertained by people of their own class in palaces or castles or mansions and were well fed. Monasteries provided shelters to the religious order while the soldiers were lodged in or tents. But the traders had to put themselves up in places "Inns" and it is they who helped develop this particular sector because they had no other alternatives. Than with the improvement of roads and transport more and more people started moving around and then to provide accommodation and food for this increasing number of travelers, many more "Inns" were set up along the frequently traveled roads and pathways. Thus the "Inn keeping" began its steady growth and became more popular. In earlier days, husband and wife team normally ran these "Inns" and they just provided basic necessities of shelter and food.

utilization of leisure created a yearning among people to travel beyond the traditional boundaries. Before the age of railroads, travelers stayed at **inns** in the country or in small hotels. The first big hotels were built in the vicinity of railroad terminals to serve the flood of new passengers.[2] These new hotels were more impersonal than the old-fashioned family-style inn or hotel. Indeed, they were usually organized as corporations in a more businesslike manner.

Vocabulary

- confer
- receiver
- psychological
- terminal
- impersonal
- security
- tangible
- physiological
- old fashioned family style inn
- provider
- intangible
- vicinity

Comprehension

1. Explain the ancient definition of hotel.
2. Explain four characteristic features of Hospitality.
3. Compare the traditional accommodation type "inns" with the modern "hotels".

Discussion

1. Think of the ways that travelers feel "a home away from home".

---

2) The cluster of hotels around Grand Central Station in New York is a good surviving example of the impact of railroads on the hotel business.

1. Types of Accommodation

A wide variety of accommodations is available to the modern tourist. They vary from the **guest house** with one or two rooms to grand luxury hotels with hundreds of rooms. A feature of Europe is the **pension**, a small establishment with perhaps ten to twenty guest rooms.[3]

The major trend in the hotel industry today is toward the large corporate-operated hotel.[4] Some of the hotel corporations operate on a **franchise** basis,[5] and the modern development in the hotel business is the **motel**.[6]

Another trend in the hotel industry is the construction of the **self-contained resort complex**. This consists of a hotel and recreational facilities, all of which in effect are isolated from the nearby community.[7] The **condominium**,[8] as a resort accommodation, has become popular

---

3) Originally, pensions offered not only lodging but also full board, all of the day's meals for the guest. Nowadays, however, most of them offer only a bed, usually at an inexpensive rate, and a "continental breakfast" of coffee and rolls.

4) A number of large companies have assumed a dominant place in the hotel industry. The biggest Holiday Inns (274,000 rooms in 1975), Sheraton, Inter-Continental, Trust Houses Forte, Hilton International, and Ramada Inns. Ownership of these hotel companies is an indication of their importance to the travel industry e.g. Hilton International owned by Trans World Airlines, Inter-Continental by Pan American Airways, and Sheraton a subsidiary of ITT.

5) The hotel and its operation are designed by the corporation, but the right to run it is sold or leased. The operator then pays a percentage to the parent corporation. The franchise can be withdrawn, however, if it does not maintain the standards that have been established.

6) A word made up from motor and hotel. The motel might best be described as a place that has accommodations both for automobiles and human beings. The typical motel is a low structure around which is built a parking lot to enable the guests to park their cars as close as possible to their rooms.

7) Examples include the holiday "villages" that have been built by Club Mediterranee for its members.

8) The condominium, as a resort accommodation, is a building or group of buildings in which individuals purchase separate units. At the same time they become joint owners of the public facilities of the structure and its grounds and recreational areas.

because of the desire of many people to own a second home for vacations.

Caravaning/camping reflects another trend in modern tourism.[9] A similar kind of arrangement, the **marina** exists for boat owners who wish to use their boats for accommodations while they are traveling in them. In recent years, resorts have been developed under the careful planning. The Costa Smeralda,[10] is the most spectacular example developing not just a resort but an entire resort area. (cf. Miami Beach)

The hotel business has its own load factor in the form of the **occupancy rate**.[11] One of the hazards of the hotel business is a high occupancy rate during one season and a very low one during another.

Vocabulary

- guest house / tourist home
- full board
- continental breakfast
- multi-national corporation
- franchise
- self-contained resort complex
- profit
- condominium
- purchase price
- maintenance cost
- syndicate
- occupancy rate
- pension
- packaged
- motel
- gambling
- joint owner
- mobile home

---

9) Cars variously called caravans, vans, or campers come equipped with sleeping quarters and even stoves and refrigerators. They are in effect small mobile homes.

10) Constructed on the Italian island of Sardinia by a syndicate headed by the Aga Khan, it contains hotels of varying price ranges, residential areas, marinas, elaborate recreational facilities, and even some light industry. The syndicate's own airline flies passengers to the island from such points as Nice and Rome. Careful planning included not only the mixture of facilities, but also the architecture and the preservation of the natural landscape.

11) This is the percentage of rooms or beds that are occupied at a certain point in time or over a period of time.

🎓 Comprehension

1. Explain the impact of railroads on the hotel business with examples.
2. Give some examples of the different varieties of accommodations available to travelers.
3. What is a franchise? Give some examples.
4. What facilities are usually available in a large, modern hotel?
5. What is a self-contained resort complex? Give examples.
6. What is the attracting feature for condominiums?
7. What is a syndicate? Provide some examples.
8. What are some examples of resort areas that do not show careful planning?
9. What is the load factor of the hotel industry called?
10. Some resorts provide special offer to overcome low occupancy in their off-season. Give some examples.

👥 Discussion

1. Franchises are one of the most popular management styles in the accommodation and catering business. Chains are also very popular. Take some examples of each term and compare similarities and differences between them.
2. If you have visited the holiday villages in Club Med, share your experience with the class.

2. Concierge

The term "concierge" first appeared in France in the Middle Ages and came to refer to the officers of the royal palace guard whose job it was to protect the king in his palace. The concierge was the holder of the keys in the royal households, with access

to all the important rooms. The concierge's responsibilities were diverse, including overseeing the administration of domestic services and performing special tasks at the request of the royal court. The definition broadened with the rise of the grand European hotels in the 16th and 17th centuries, though it was not until the mid-20th century that the concierge became a must-have feature of North American hotels.

The concierge[12] usually identified by his uniform bearing golden cross-keys insignia on both lapels, performs various functions for the guests, such as management of the room keys, handling of mail and messages or packages, booking for train and theater tickets, taking care of complaints or problems, answering questions and giving advices about nearly everything; A unique combination of clerk, secretary, manager, adviser and information center.

So prestigious is the concierge that there is an association, from France, dedicated specifically to hotel concierges, Les Clefs d'Or, whose motto is "service through friendship". Today their membership numbers more than 3,500 concierges representing 37 countries. Members are distinguished by the gold keys they display on their lapels."

Les Clefs D'Or or Golden Keys, the

---

12) The term concierge evolved from the French Comte Des Cierges, the Keeper of the Candles, who tended to visiting nobles in castles of the medieval era.

symbol of Concierges all over the world

📓 Vocabulary

- concierge
- prestigious
- insignia
- lapel

🎓 Comprehension

1. When you're staying at a hotel, you need some information around the area. Who will be the contact person in the hotel, and what is this person called?
2. What is the symbol of the concierge?
3. What is origin of the term "concierge"?

Catering

Catering is the business of providing food service at a remote site or a site such as a hotel, public house (pub), or other location. An organization providing Food and Beverage is called a catering establishment. Catering establishments are broadly classified into the primary catering establishment and the secondary catering establishment. Hotel, Restaurants and fast food outlets, which are primarily concerned with the provision of food and beverage as a main source of revenue, are called primary catering establishment. The provision of food and beverage is also a part of another business such as welfare catering and industrial catering, which is secondary catering establishment (partly excepted from en.wikipedia.org).

Types of Catering Establishment

Catering typically refers to off-premise service, and provides food and drink for transients. Food services are a typical feature of hotels. The main purpose of hotels is to provide accommodation, but the service of food and beverage may be included as a part of business. Hotels provide not only room service to the guest's room, but also other catering service through a number of outlets such as the coffee shop, room service, banquets, specialty restaurant, grill room, and cocktail bars.

Restaurants are of various standards e.g. a specialty or an A graded restaurants; they offer a wide choice from an elaborate menu and a very high quality of service.

Bars & Pubs is the concept of public houses in England. They are geared to provide service of all types of alcohol with an emphasis on draught beer and good music. Foods may also be served from a limited menu.

Fast food restaurant is basically an American concept. The service of food & beverage is at a faster pace than an "a la cart Restaurant" as the menu is compiled with a special emphasis on the speed of preparation and service.

Outdoor catering means catering to a large number of people at a venue of their choice. Hotels, restaurants and catering contractors meet this growing demand. The types of food and set-up depend entirely on the price agreed upon outdoor catering, such as marriages parties and convention.

Foodservice (US English) is also distinguished by commercial foodservice and non-commercial foodservice; commercial foodservice comprises operations whose primary business is food and beverage, and non-commercial foodservice where food and beverages are served, but are not the primary business. Commercial operators make up the largest segment of F&B with just over 80% market share (Restaurants Canada, 2014). It is made up of quick-service restaurants (QSRs), full-service restaurants, catering, and drinking establishments.

Types of Commercial Foodservice Operators

Fine dining restaurants are characterized by highly trained chefs preparing complex food items, exquisitely presented. Meals are brought to the table by experienced servers with sound food and beverage knowledge in an upscale atmosphere with table linens, fine china, crystal stemware, and silver-plate cutlery. The table is often embellished with fresh flowers and candles.

Family/casual restaurants are characterized by being open for all three meal periods. These operations offer affordable menu items that span a variety of customer tastes. They also have the operational flexibility in menu and restaurant layout to welcome large groups of diners.

Ethnic restaurants typically reflect the owner's cultural identity. While these restaurants are popular with many markets, they are often particularly of interest to visitors and new immigrants looking for a specific environment and other people with whom they have a shared culture. Food is often the medium for this sense of belonging (Koc & Welsh, 2001; Laroche, Kim, Tomiuk, & Belisle, 2005).

Food, in fact, may be one of the reasons that people travel. Foodservice providers also service the visitor market, which presents unique challenges as guests will bring with them the tastes and eating habits of their home country or region (partly excerpted from Briscoe & Tripp 2012)

As Rebecca Melnyk (2016) mentions, "Food, as a part of retail, is becoming more and more relevant for creating memorable experiences." Many people visit France, for example, because of the **gourmet** meals. Similarly, the excellent restaurants of Hong Kong constitute one of its principal tourist attractions.

The accommodations and catering service industries employ large numbers of people.[13] This intensive use of labor is attractive to developing countries. Furthermore, many of the hotel and restaurant jobs are semi-skilled work, so only a small amount of training is necessary to fill them.

Vocabulary

• provision	• a la cart Restaurant	• room service
• snack bar	• gourmet	• delicatessens
• liquor	• semiskilled work	

---

13) At a luxury hotel, there may be as many as two or three employees for every guest room. At a large commercial hotel, there are usually about eight employees for every ten guest rooms.

🎓 Comprehension

1. What is the catering establishment?
2. Give examples of primary catering establishments and secondary catering establishments.
3. What is the difference between primary catering and secondary catering?
4. What catering services are available?

👥 Discussion

1. France is famous for gourmet dishes. Name some of them.
2. Tourism is often called a labor-intensive business. Take some examples and show the ratio of hotel employees to hotel rooms.
3. What is the reason that makes tourism attractive in the developing countries?

V

PART

Culture

1

Overview of Culture

The modern term "culture" is based on a term used by the Ancient Roman orator Cicero, where he wrote of a cultivation of the soul or "*cultura animi*", using an agricultural metaphor for the development of a philosophical soul. Samuel Pufendorf took over this metaphor in a modern context, "*referring to all the ways in which human beings overcome their original barbarism, and through artifice, become fully human.*" **Culture**, originally meant 'cultivate' is a term that has many different meanings. When the concept first emerged in 18C, it connoted a process of cultivation or improvement, as in agriculture. In 19C, it came to refer to the betterment or refinement of the individual, especially through education.[1] In 20C, culture emerged as a concept central to anthropology, encompassing all human phenomena.[2]

As described by Velkley (2002), the term "culture," which originally

---

1) In the 19th century, humanists such as English poet and essayist Matthew Arnold (1822–1888) used the word "culture" to refer to an ideal of individual human refinement, of "the best that has been thought and said in the world."

2) Specifically, culture in American anthropology had two meanings: (1) the evolved human capacity to classify and represent experiences with symbols, and (2) the distinct ways that people living in different parts of the world classified and represented their experiences.

meant the cultivation of the soul or mind, acquires most of its later modern meanings in the writings of the 18th-century German thinkers, who were on various levels developing Rousseau's criticism of "modern liberalism and enlightenment." Thus a contrast between "culture" and "civilization" is usually implied in these authors, even when not expressed as such. Two primary meanings of culture emerge from this period: culture as the folk-spirit having a unique identity and culture as cultivation of way-wardness or free individuality. The first meaning is predominant in our current use of the term "**culture**," although the second still plays a large role in what we think culture should achieve, namely the full "expression" of the unique or "authentic" self (partly excerpted from en.wikipedia.org).

Vocabulary

- cultivation
- philosophical
- emerge
- refinement
- phenomena
- authentic

- agricultural
- barbarism
- improvement
- anthropology
- compile

- metaphor
- artifice
- betterment
- encompass
- predominant

Comprehension

1. The term "culture" has a metaphoric meaning of agriculture. Explain the metaphoric sense of culture and its origin.
2. Explain two primary meanings of culture in the 21st Century.

2

Cultural Iceberg

In 1976, Hall developed the iceberg analogy of culture. If the culture of a society was the iceberg, there are some aspects visible, above the water, but there is a larger portion hidden beneath the surface. The external, or conscious, part of culture is what we can see and is the tip of the iceberg and includes behaviors and some beliefs. The internal, or subconscious, part of culture is below the surface of a society and includes some beliefs and the values and thought patterns that underlie behavior. There are major differences between the conscious and unconscious culture.

Internal	vs	External
Implicitly Learned		Explicitly Learned
Unconscious		Conscious
Difficult to Change		Easily Changed
Subjective Knowledge		Objective Knowledge

Hall suggests that the only way to learn the internal culture of others is to actively participate in their culture. When one first enters a new culture, only the most overt behaviors are apparent. As one spends more time in that new culture, the underlying beliefs, values, and thought patterns that dictate that behavior will be uncovered. What this model teaches us is that we cannot judge a new culture based only on what we see when we first enter it. We must take the time to get to know individuals from that culture and interact with them. Only by doing so can we uncover the values and beliefs that underlie the behavior of that society. (www.constantforeigner.com ©2010)

Culture is a broad and general term to include various parts of one society. The comprehensive definition of culture can be developed only when we consider various parts of culture. The given sectors are parts of culture, and refers to the ways of life, which includes but not limited to:

Language: the oldest human institution and the most sophisticated medium of expression.

Arts & Sciences: the most advanced and refined forms of human expression.

Thought: the ways in which people perceive, interpret, and understand the world around them.

Spirituality: the value system transmitted through generations for the inner well-being of human beings, expressed through language and actions.

Social activity: the shared pursuits within a cultural community, demonstrated in a variety of festivities and life-celebrating events.

Interaction: the social aspects of human contact, including the give-and-take of socialization, negotiation, protocol, and conventions.

All of the above collectively define the meaning of Culture.

Vocabulary

• visible	• surface	• apparent
• interact	• sophisticate	• refine
• pursuit	• demonstrate	• collectively

🎓 Comprehension

1. Explain the analogy between the icebergs of the culture.
2. According to Hall (1976), the culture has two parts, the external and/ or the internal part. Compare the two parts of culture, and give some examples of them.
3. Culture refers to the ways of life, and it includes many aspects such as language, artifacts, ways of thinking, etc. Give some examples of each sub-areas of culture.
    a. How does the language express the culture of the society?
    b. How do the arts and science express the culture of one society?
    c. The way of thinking is affected by the culture. How does the thought affect perceiving, interpreting, and understanding the world?
    d. The spirituality is the value system of the culture. What could be the main value of our society?
    e. The social activity is a form of communal activities. This includes festivals and events. Choose one of those activities and explain it from the angles of culture.
    f. The styles of interaction are different from culture to culture. It is manifested through socialization, negotiation, conventions, etc. Think of the interaction style of Koreans.

Definitions of Culture

Culture embodies the social phenomenon, thus it needs a comprehensive definition to cover all the phenomenon of one society. Kroeber and Kluckhohn compiled a list of 164 definitions of "culture" in *Culture: A Critical Review of Concepts and Definitions* in 1952. The following extracts provide the varied perspective of culture, and its characteristics.

Culture consists of patterns, explicit and implicit, of and for behavior acquired and transmitted by symbols, constituting the distinctive achievement of human groups, including their embodiments in artifacts; the essential core of culture consists of traditional ideas and especially their attached values; culture systems may, on the one hand, be considered as products of action, on the other hand, as conditioning influences upon further action. (Kroeber & Kluckhohn 1952; Hofstede 1997)

Culture is a collective programming of the mind that distinguishes the members of one group or category of people from another. (Kluckhohn, & Kelly 1945; Hofstede 1997)

Culture is communication, communication is culture. (Hall 1959; 1983)

Culture is the systems of knowledge shared by a relatively large group of people. (Gudykunst and Kim 1992)

Culture refers to the cumulative deposit of knowledge, experience, beliefs, values, attitudes, meanings, hierarchies, religion, notions of time, roles, spatial relations, concepts of the universe, and material objects and possessions acquired by a group of people in the course of generations through individual and group striving. (Samovar and Porter 1994; Hofstede 1997)

Culture is a way of life of a group of people - the behaviors, beliefs, values, and symbols that they accept, generally without thinking about them, and that are passed along by communication and imitation from one generation to the next. (Hofstede and Hofstede 2005)

Culture is the sum of total of the learned behavior of a group of people that are generally considered to be the tradition of that people and are transmitted from generation to generation.

👥 Discussion

Define culture in your own words.

Culture is _____

because _____.

4

Cultural Determinism & Cultural Relativism

The position that the ideas, meanings, beliefs and values people learn as members of society determines human nature. People are what they learn. Optimistic version of cultural determinism place no limits on the abilities of human beings to do or to be whatever they want. Some anthropologists suggest that there is no universal "right way" of being human. "Right way" is almost always "our way"; that "our way" in one society almost never corresponds to "our way" in any other society. Proper attitude of an informed human being could only be that of tolerance.

Different cultural groups think, feel, and act differently. There is no scientific standards for considering one group as intrinsically superior or inferior to another. Studying differences in culture among groups and societies presupposes a position of cultural relativism. Information about the nature of cultural differences between societies, their roots, and their consequences should precede judgment and action. Negotiation is more likely to succeed when the parties concerned understand the reasons for the differences in viewpoints.

Vocabulary

- optimistic
- intrinsically
- precede
- determinism
- presuppose
- negotiation
- tolerance
- relativism

Comprehension

1. What is the right way of human beings?
2. Before you judge other cultures, you should do _____ .
3. What is cultural relativism?

Ethnocentrism

Ethnocentrism[3] is the belief that one's own culture is superior to that of other cultures. It occurs when one culture or nation places itself at the top of an imagined hierarchy of cultures and nations and subsequently assigns other cultures and nations equivalent or lower value on that scale. However, it is not unusual for a person to consider that whatever they believe is the most appropriate system of belief or that however they behave is the most appropriate and "natural" behavior. Ethnocentrism leads us to make false assumptions about cultural differences. We are ethnocentric when we use our cultural norms to make generalizations about other peoples' cultures and customs. Such generalizations — often made without a conscious awareness that we've used our culture as a universal yardstick — can be way off base and cause us to misjudge other peoples. It is a form of reductionism that reduces the "other way" of life to a distorted version of one's own. Ethnocentrism distorts communication between human beings,

---

3) The term ethnocentrism was coined by William G. Sumner, upon observing the tendency for people to differentiate between the in-group and others. He described it as often leading to pride, vanity, beliefs of one's own group's superiority, and contempt of outsiders. The word ethnocentrism derives from the Greek word ethnos, meaning "nation" or "people," and the English word center. A common idiom for ethnocentrism is "tunnel vision."

creating conflicts and inhibiting resolution of conflicts. This is particularly important in case of global interaction.

📖 Vocabulary

- ethnocentrism
- subsequently
- appropriate
- reductionism
- superior
- assign
- assumption
- inhibit
- hierarchy
- equivalent
- norm
- resolution

🎓 Comprehension

1. What is ethnocentrism?
2. Read the following passages and give some examples of ethnocentrism.
   a. Ethnocentrism found in languages
   b. Ethnocentrism found in mythologies
   c. Ethnocentrism found in food preferences

[Ethnocentrism]

Culture shock can be an excellent lesson in relative values and in understanding human differences. The reason culture shock occurs is that we are not prepared for these differences. Because of the way we are taught our culture, we are all ethnocentric. This term comes from the Greek root ethnos, meaning a people or group. Thus, it refers to the fact that our outlook or world view is centered on our own way of life. Ethnocentrism is the belief that one's own patterns of behavior are the best: the most nature, beautiful, right, or important. Therefore, other people, to the extent that they live differently, live by standards that are inhuman, irrational, unnatural, or wrong.

Ethnocentrism is the view that one's own culture is better than all others; it is the way all people feel about themselves as compared to outsiders. There is no one in our society who is not ethnocentric to some degree, no matter how liberal ad open-minded he or she might claim to be. People will always find some aspect of another culture distasteful, be it sexual practices, a way of treating friends or relatives, or simply a food that they cannot manage to get down with a smile. This is not something we should be ashamed of, because it is a natural outcome of growing up in any society. However, as anthropologists who study other cultures, it is something we should constantly be aware of, so that when we are tempted to make value judgments about another way of life, we can look at the situation objectively and take our bias into account.

Ethnocentrism can be seen in many aspects of culture—myths, folktales, proverbs, and even language. For example, in many languages, especially those of non-Western societies, the word used to refer to one's own tribe or ethnic group literally means "mankind" or "human". This implies that members of other groups are less than human. For example, the term eskimo, used to refer to groups that inhabit the arctic and subarctic regions, is an Indian word used by neighbors of the Eskimos who observed their strange way of life but did not share it. The term means "eaters of raw flesh," and as such is an ethnocentric observation about cultural practices that were normal to one group and repulsive to another. On the other hand, if we look at one subgroup among the Alaskan natives we find them calling themselves inuit, which means "real people" (they obviously did not think eating raw flesh was anything out of the ordinary). Here, then, is a contrast between one's own group, which is real, and the rest of the world, which not so "real." Both terms, eskimo and inuit, are equally ethnocentric — one as an observation about differences, the other as a self-evaluation. However, inuit is now seen as a more appropriate term because of its origin.

Another example of ethnocentrism in language can be found in the origin of the English term barbarian. Originally a Greek word, the term was used to refer to tribes that lived around the edge of ancient Greek society. The Greeks referred to these people as barbars because they could not understand their speech. Bar-bar was the Greek word for the sound a dog makes, like our word bow-wow. The Greeks, in a classic example of ethnocentrism, considered those whose speech they could not understand to be on the same level as dogs, which also could not be understood. They did not grant such people the status of human being, much as the word Eskimo gives those people subhuman status.

Shifting from language to myths and folktales, we find a good example of ethnocentrism in the creation myth of the Cherokee Indians. According to this story, the Creator made three clay images of a man and baked them in an oven. In his haste to admire his handiwork, he took the first image out of the oven before it was fully baked and found that it was too pale. He waited a while and then removed the second image; it was just right, a full reddish-brown hue. He was so pleased with his work that he sat there and admired it, completely forgetting about the third image. Finally he smelled it burning, but by the time he could rescue it from the oven it had already been burnt, and it came out completely black!

Food preferences are perhaps the most familiar aspect of ethnocentrism. Every culture has developed preferences for certain kinds of food and drink, and equally strong attitudes toward others. It is interesting to note that much of this ethnocentrism is in our heads and not in our tongues, for something can taste delicious until we are told what it is. We have all heard stories about people being fed a meal of snake or horse meat or something equally repugnant in American culture and commenting on how tasty it was — until they were told what they had just eaten, upon which they turned green and hurriedly asked to be excused from the table.

Certain food preferences seem natural to us. We usually do not recognize that they are natural only because we have grown up with them; they are quite likely to be unnatural to someone from a different culture. In Southeast Asia, for example, the majority of adults do not drink milk. To many Americans it is inconceivable that people in other parts of the world do not drink milk, since to us it is a "natural" food. In China, a dog meat is a delicacy; but the thought of eating a dog is enough to make most Americans feel sick.

Yet we can see how this is a part of a cultural pattern. Americans keep dogs as pets and tend to think of dogs as almost human. Therefore, we would not dream of eating dog meat. Horse, too, sometimes become pets, and horse meat is also rejected by most Americans, although not because of its taste. You may have eaten it without knowing it, and you probably would not recognize it if someone didn't tell you what you were eating.

On the other hand, we generally do not feel affection for cows or pigs, and we eat their meat without any feeling of regret. In India, a cow receives the kind of care that a horse or even a dog receives in our country, and the attitude of Indians toward eating beef is similar to our feeling about eating dog meat. On the other hand, in China dogs are not treated as kindly as they are in the United States. Since they are not pets, the attitude of Chinese people toward dogs is similar to our attitude toward cows. (From *Mosaic*, pp. 197-200)

6

Cultural Layers

National culture is the sum total of the *beliefs, rituals, rules, customs, artifacts,* and *institutions* that characterize the population. A nation's *culture* and *sub-cultures* affect how organizational transactions are conducted. A society's values have an impact on organizational values because of the interactive nature of work, leisure, family, and community. Learning to operate in the national culture is becoming a requirement for effective management and communication.

Hofstede (1980:25) mentions that Culture is a mental programming. According to Hofstede, culture is the "collective programming of the mind, which distinguishes the members of one category of people from another." Any culture programmed in an organization is not separate, because any change of cultural programs is always taking place within formal and informal strategic planning processes.

Hofstede also divided culture into four layers (or four main elements): symbols, heroes, rituals and values. It is critical for organizational managers, because it can affect business or operation at different degree and in different ways. An onion diagram model of organizational culture developed by Hofstede (1997:9) is presented here (Figure 1).

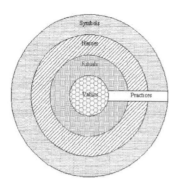

Figure 1. Onion Diagram:
Manifestation of Culture at
Different Levels

Cultural differences manifest themselves in different ways and differing levels of depth. Symbols represent the most superficial and values the deepest manifestations of culture, with heroes and rituals in between.

Symbols are words, gestures, pictures, or objects that carry a particular meaning which is only recognized by those who share a particular culture. New symbols easily develop, old ones disappear. Symbols from one particular group are regularly copied by others. This is why symbols represent the outermost layer of a culture.

Heroes are persons, past or present, real or fictitious, who possess characteristics that are highly prized in a culture. They also serve as models for behavior.

Rituals are collective activities, sometimes superfluous in reaching desired objectives, but are considered as socially essential. They are therefore carried out most of the times for their own sake (ways of greetings, paying respect to others, religious and social ceremonies, etc.).

The core of a culture is formed by **values**. They are broad tendencies for preferences of certain state of affairs to others (good-evil, right-wrong, natural-unnatural). Many values remain unconscious to those who hold them. Therefore they often cannot be discussed, nor can they be directly observed by others. Values can only be inferred from the way people act under different circumstances.

Symbols, heroes, and rituals are the tangible or visual aspects of the practices of a culture. The true cultural meaning of the practices is intangible; this is revealed only when the practices are interpreted by the insiders.

Vocabulary

- organizational
- onion diagram model

- transactions
- superfluous

Comprehension

1. Explain Hofstede(1997)'s Onion Model of culture.
2. Give some examples of each layer of culture.

Discussion

1. With Hofstede's Onion Model, let us talk about Korean culture.

7

Cultural Dimensions

Hofstede (1997) has devised a technique to measure cultural differences among different societies, and provides a framework for cross-cultural communication.[4] The original theory proposed four dimensions along which cultural values could be analyzed: individualism-collectivism; uncertainty avoidance; power distance (strength of social hierarchy) and masculinity-femininity (task orientation versus person-orientation).[5]

Power distance: The level of acceptance by a society of the unequal distribution of power in organizations. The index measures the degree of inequality that exists in a society. In higher power distance cultures, employees acknowledge the boss's authority and follow the chain of

---

4) Hofstede developed the cultural dimensional model to examine the results of a world-wide survey of employee values by IBM in the 1960s and 1970s. The theory was one of the first that could be quantified, and could be used to explain observed differences between cultures. (wikipedia)

5) Independent research in Hong Kong led Hofstede to add a fifth dimension, long-term orientation, to cover aspects of values not discussed in the original paradigm. In the 2010 edition of *Cultures and Organizations:Software of the Mind,* Hofstede added a sixth dimension, indulgence versus self-restraint, as a result of co-author Michael Minkov's analysis of data from the World Values Survey. (wikipedia)

command. The result is a more centralized authority and structure

Uncertainty avoidance: The index measures the extent to which people in a society feels threatened by uncertain or ambiguous situations. Countries with a high level of uncertainty avoidance tend to have specific rules, laws, and procedures. Managers in these countries tend towards low-risk decision-making, and employees exhibit little aggressiveness.

Individualism: The index measure the tendency of people to fend for themselves and their family. In countries that value individualism, individual initiative and achievement are highly valued and the relationship of the individual with organizations is one of independence. Individualism refers to a loosely knit social framework in a society in which people are supposed to take care of themselves and their immediate families only. The other end of the spectrum would be collectivism that occurs when there is a tight social framework in which people distinguish between in-groups and out-groups; they expect their in-groups (relatives, clans, organizations) to look after them in exchange for absolute loyalty.

Masculinity (Achievement vs. Relationship): The index measures the extent to which assertiveness and materialism is valued (achievement). In highly masculine societies, there is considerable job stress and conflict between job and family roles. The other end of the spectrum would be femininity (relationship).

In the area of organizational culture, further sophistication was introduced by Schein (2010)[6] with the concept of time. He identifies three types of organization depending on their time orientation: past, present and future.[7] Another dimension for how we relate to time is the notion of monochronic and polychronic. Monochronic is a view of linear time that can be split, wasted, spent etc. This is typical of the western rational cultures. Some culture in Southern Europe or Middle East view time as *polychronic, a kind of medium defined more by what is accomplished than by a clock, within*

---

6) Schein, Edgar H. *Organization Culture and Leadership* (Jossey-Bass)

7) Hofstede again has found that economic development was correlated with a **future** orientation.

which several things can be done simultaneously. In polychronic cultures, relationships are viewed as more important than short-run efficiency and may leave monochronic managers frustrated and impatient.

Vocabulary

- Individualism
- collectivism
- uncertainty avoidance
- masculinity
- femininity
- authority
- aggressiveness
- spectrum
- in-groups
- out-groups
- assertiveness
- materialism
- monochronic
- polychronic

Comprehension

1. In cross-cultural communication, explain how cultural differences can be measured.
2. Evaluate Korean culture based on the 4 cultural dimensions of Hofstede.
3. Explain the difference in perceiving time.
4. Evaluate Korean's time perception based on Schein's division.

Discussion

1. Compare Korean culture with other cultures using the cultural dimensional model.

Cultural Awareness

Cultural Awareness

It is probably necessary to identify the cultural differences that may exist between one's home country and the country of business operation. Where the differences exist, one must decide whether and to what extent the home-country practices may be adapted to the foreign environment. Most of the times the differences are not very apparent or tangible. Certain aspects of a culture may be learned consciously (e.g. methods of greeting people), some other differences are learned subconsciously (e.g. methods of problem solving).

It's fairly well accepted that with each passing day, societies and organizations are becoming less homogenous and we find ourselves dealing with cultural diversity in many more places of our lives. From our neighborhoods and schools to our workplaces and virtual communities, we are much more likely to interact with people who are different from ourselves. There are similarities, too, of course; yet it is the ability to discern which differences are making a difference, that is the key to fulfilling the promise of global diversity.

We define diversity as the differences that exist within us all, that bring a variety of backgrounds, styles, perspectives, values, and beliefs as assets to groups and organizations. Workforce diversity includes many dimensions in which people are different from age, ethnicity, race, nationality, gender, and religion to belief systems, role and organizational status, geographic location, native language, socioeconomics, income level, education, personality, professional experience, and work style. But diversity is always there and it's always having an impact - whether people and systems are aware (conscious) of it or not (unconscious.) The building of cultural awareness may not be an easy task, but once accomplished, it definitely helps a job done efficiently in a foreign environment.
(www.languageandculture.com)

Cultural Clustering

Some countries may share many attributes that help mold their cultures (the modifiers may be language, religion, geographical location, etc.). Countries may be grouped by similarities in values and attitudes, which makes the cultural clustering. Fewer differences may be expected when moving within a cluster than when moving from one cluster to another.
(http://www.tamu.edu)

Vocabulary

• apparent	• tangible	• consciously
• subconsciously	• attribute	• modifier
• cluster	• awareness	

Comprehension

1. What is cultural awareness?
2. What is cultural clustering?
3. What are the variables for forming the clustering?

CHAPTER 9

Culture & Language

There is a unique tie between culture and language. The languages we speak provide us with the words and concepts to describe the world around us, allowing us to verbalize certain values easily. Anything we assume as a group cultural value will surely have a known and easily understandable term. The English word "privacy" and the Chinese word "關系 (guanxi)" both have clear and strong meanings in their respective languages, but are not necessarily found in all other languages. Being a native speaker of one's mother tongue brings with it more than just the ability to communicate, it brings with it the ability to understand why someone thinks and acts as they do.

Even within a language, certain terms may only be used by certain groups and this jargon or vernacular can quickly reflect what the group values. If you regularly use the term "return on investment", this says a great deal about what you value in your role at an organization. Similarly, if you immediately understand the complexities and nuances of the term "sustainable development," then you too belong to a group of people who undoubtedly share a culture and worldview.

Languages also have differing structures that can reinforce and contribute to our worldview and cultural beliefs. Take, for example, languages such as French that quickly and easily differentiate between a "formal" and "informal" relationship with others, depending on which form of the word "you" is used. In learning this language as a child, you are taught that an appropriate way to demonstrate respect to certain other people is in word choice and because this is part of how you must speak, it becomes part of how you must think.

These differences in language, reflective of our different cultures, are at the core of what makes translation of a text from one language to another often times difficult. Words can have deep meaning, and finding the right word for the right context can be an interesting and formidable challenge. (www.languageandculture.com)

Vocabulary

- mother tongue
- nuances
- jargon
- formidable
- vernacular
- worldview

Comprehension

1. Explain the respective meaning of the English word "privacy" and the Chinese word "關系 (guanxi)" and construe these terms in your own culture.
2. Depending on the situation, the language can be differentiated either formal or informal. Give some examples.
3. Language can reflect the value you belong to. Give some examples.

[Native Americans]

When I was about five years old, I used to watch a bird in the skies of southern Alberta from the Blackfeet Blood Reserve in northern Montana where I was born. I loved this bird; I would watch him for hours. He would glide effortlessly in that gigantic sky, or he would come down and light on the water and float there very majestically. Sometimes when I watched him he would creep into the grasses and waddle around not very gracefully. We called him meksikatsi, which in the Blackfeet language means "pink-colored feet"; meksikatsi and I became very good friends.

The bird had a very particular significance to me because I desperately wanted to be able to fly too. I felt very much as if I was the kind of person who had been born into a world where flight was impossible, and most of the things that I dreamed about or read about would not be possible for me but would be possible only for other people.

When I was ten years old, my life changed drastically. I found myself adopted forcefully and against my parents' will; they were considered inadequate parents because they could not make enough money to support me, so I found myself in that terrible position that 60 percent of Native Americans find themselves in: living in a city that they do not understand at all, not in another culture but between two cultures.

A teacher of the English language told me that meksikatsi was not called meksikatsi, even though that is what my people had called that bird for thousands of years. Meksikatsi, he said, was really "duck." I was very disappointed with English. I could not understand it. First of all, the bird didn't look like "duck," and when it made a noise it didn't sound like "duck," and I was even more confused when I found out that the meaning of the verb "to duck" came from the bird and not vice versa.

This was the beginning of a very complex lesson for me that doesn't just happen to black, Chicano, Jewish, and Indian children but to all children. We are born into a cultural preconception that we call reality and that we never question. We essentially know the world in terms of that cultural package or preconception, and we are so unaware of it that the most liberal of us go through life with a kind of ethnocentricity that automatically rules out all other ways of seeing the world.

As I came to understand English better, I understood that it made a great deal of sense, but I never forgot that meksikatsi made a different kind of sense. I realized that languages are not just different words for the same things but totally different concepts, totally different ways of experiencing and looking at the world.

As artists have always known, reality depends entirely on how you see things. I grew up in a place that was called a wilderness, but I could never understand how that amazing ecological park could be called "wilderness," something wild that needs to be harnessed. Nature is some sort of foe, some sort of adversary, in the dominant culture's mentality. We are not part of nature in this society; we are created above it, outside of it, and feel that we must dominate and change it before we can be comfortable and safe within it. I grew up in a culture that considers us literally a part of the entire process that is called nature, to such an extent that when Black Elk called himself the brother of the bear, he was quite serious. In other words, Indians did not need Darwin to find out that they were part of nature.

I saw my first wilderness, as I recall, one August day when I got off a Greyhound bus in a city called New York. Now that struck me as being fairly wild and pretty much out of hand. But I did not understand how the term could be applied to the place where I was from.

Gradually, through the help of some very unusual teachers, I was able to find my way into two cultures rather than remain helplessly between two cultures. The earth is such an important symbol to most primal people that when we use European languages we tend to capitalize the E in much the same way that the word God is capitalized by people in the dominant culture. You can imagine my distress when I was ten years old to find out that synonyms for the word earth—dirt and soil—were used to describe uncleanliness on the one hand and obscenity on the other. I could not possibly understand how something that could be dirty could have any kind of negative connotations. It would be like saying the person is godly, so don't go near him, and I could not grasp how these ideas made their way into the English language.

Jamake Highwater

10

Culture & Values

Culture is the sum of learned beliefs, values, and customs that regulate the behavior of members of a particular society. Beliefs and values are guides of behavior and customs are acceptable ways of behaving. A belief is an opinion that reflects a person's particular knowledge and assessment of an issue. Values are general statements that guide behavior and influence beliefs and attitudes. A value system helps people choose between alternatives in everyday life. Customs are overt modes of behavior that constitute culturally approved ways of behaving in specific situations. Customs vary among countries, regions, and even families. Dominant cultural values are referred to as core values; they tend to affect and reflect the core character of a particular society. Core values are slow and difficult to change.

📖 Vocabulary

- regulate
- alternatives
- assessment
- core values

🎓 Comprehension

1. A person's behavior is guided by _____ and the acceptable way of behaving is _____ .

2. What are your dominant cultural values?

[Traditional American Value]

Traditional American value which influence how and why Americans do things include individual freedom, equality of opportunity, material wealth, self-reliance, competition, and hard work. These are core American values. Understanding these values can help one understand American beliefs that may be very different to those held in Korea.

Individual Freedom and Self-Reliance

The colonists who left England wanted to be able to control their own lives and destiny without the interference from a king or other aristocrats. Some also felt that religion should not play a part in deciding matters of state. When the constitution was written in 1789, they separated church and state so that there would never be a government-supported church. This placed a great deal of limitation on the power and influence that the church could impose in America. Hence, the colonists ensured that neither religion nor an aristocracy would develop into power in America. There would be no ruling class in this new nation.

This act had a profound effect on the American culture, since it was the first country to allow its citizens to make decisions on matters of state. This created a climate of freedom, but also placed an emphasis on the individual. One could not depend on the state alone to provide a standard of living. It was up to the individual himself to create his own.

The price paid for this individual freedom is self-reliance. If individuals were not able to rely on themselves, they would lose their freedom. This meant achieving both financial and emotional independence from one's parents and family as soon as possible. Most Americans are expected to become independent between the ages of 18 and 21. Americans believe that they should be able to solve their own problems, stand on their own feet and be able to take care of themselves.

This strong belief in self-reliance continues today as a fundamental American value. Young Americans search for employment during their teens and sometimes in childhood to obtain some form of financial independence from their parents. If they are dependent on their parents, they feel they have lost the freedom to do as they wish. Also, people who are dependent often lose respect from their peers since dependence is associated with weakness.

Even if Americans are not fully independent, they try at all costs to appear so. To have power and respect in America, individuals must be seen as self-reliant. Receiving aid in the form of handouts, charity or government support is not admired and often discouraged. Americans feel that accepting charity openly sets a dad example and develops a dependent society that is unable to function on its own. In short, Americans feel that people should be able to take care of themselves without extended help from others.

Equality of Opportunity and Competition

Everyone has a chance to succeed in America. This has been the case from the early settlers to immigrants arriving today. Many feel that with the freedom to express religious, political opinions with little social control, they have a better chance of personal success.

Without an aristocracy, there were no preset limits on opportunity and power. Many immigrants who came to America did have their dreams fulfilled. This created a new class system in America known as the upper/middle/lower classes. The wealthy were deemed to be upper class, while the poor were lower class.

Traditionally, one was unable to change classes in Europe, but in America a person's hard work could make them successful enough in wealth and power to change classes. The idea of equality of opportunity was critical for this to be possible.

One must understand that when Americans say they believe in equality of opportunity, they do not mean that everyone is equal. They mean that everyone should have an equal chance of success. Hence, it is often a race to see who is able to beat the other in succeeding. This is an ethical rule that Americans hold to ensure that opportunities for advancement in society are given out fairly, not just because one was born into a wealthier family than the other or because one practices a certain religion while another does not. Hence, the American view of fair play may be viewed as a providing a foundation for a plural society to function together in peace. If one group of people does not see bias favoring the other, then there is no reason for hostility or anger towards another people. Society can settle their differences with competition between themselves instead of blaming a flawed and biased system of government.

Competition is the price that Americans pay for the chance of equal opportunity. Each American is competition with each other at intelligence, strength, agility, creativity and drive. Americans are always competing against each other in contests seeking success to add to their merit.

People who are successful are deemed winners in society, while those who continually fail to succeed are viewed as losers in American society. Americans do not think highly of those who are considered losers, and the competition to be a winner starts early in school. Competition is encouraged and fostered by schools and community groups.

The pressure to compete makes Americans look energetic, but is also physically and mentally demanding. Being able to contribute to society is highly regarded in American culture. A problem arises for most American after they retire and are no longer competing within society. Many

Americans view older Americans over 65 as no longer useful to American society since they are no longer contribution or competing. Hence, many retired Americans do not fit into the accepted mainstream American life as well as those who are employed.

Material Wealth and Hard Work

Being a land of opportunity also held a true belief in America. If one works hard, they will gain material wealth. Many immigrants became rich from their hard work in America, hence coining the term rags to riches. The American dream where one could work and improve their lives was very alluring to immigrants worldwide. They achieved material wealth and became a value to the American people. the amount of material wealth one had represented how successful they were independently in being able to stand on their own feel and create a life for themselves.

American cultural value on wealth is called materialism. This was because wealth was the traditional measure of social status in America. Since there was no aristocracy or title, the only measure of one's worth was through their possessions. In some cases, the desire for material success was based on religious values. The puritans who colonized America felt that God rewarded a strong work ethic with material wealth. Hence, material success was associated with Godliness.

The price to pay for material wealth is hard work. Only with hard work could the settles convert the resources from the ground into material wealth to provide a more comfortable standard of living. Americans also value their possessions as valuable because they are representative of their hard work and physical abilities.

As America is changing from an industrial based economy to a service and information economy, the chances of achieving the traditional American dream are becoming fewer. There are fewer higher paying jobs available to the public and greater competition between job seekers. Factory workers are now paid less and it is becoming harder and harder to go from "rags to riches." Americans are working longer hours for less money and the income gap between rich and poor is increasing. The reality is now that hard work no longer means you will be able to accumulate material wealth or rewards.

Most Americans still believe in the concept of hard work, since it is necessary to be competitive within American society. Those who are not competitive are shunned by society if they receive government assistance known as welfare payments.

America today is facing a crisis within its workforce. There is now a large difference dream and the reality of the American economy. Equality of opportunity is not always practiced. Many wealthy families have an advantage in competition by being able to send their children to better schools, hence a better chance of success.

Most black Americans have fewer opportunities than white Americans, and immigrants today have fewer opportunities than those who came before them. This is because the traditional opportunities of employment are becoming fewer and fewer. Plus higher paying positions require a high level of education which most poor families cannot afford.

Even so, those who study hard are able to compete in school and succeed. They will find a successful place in American culture. If we understand the fundamental values which Americans hold, we can understand how they have influenced how Americans act in everyday life and in the world around them.

Attractions and Cultural Events

Attractions

People travel for any number of reasons, and any place can become a tourist destination as long as it is different from the place where the traveler usually lives, e.g. large cities like London, Paris, New York, and Tokyo; seashore areas in warm climates like the Caribbean[1] and the Mediterranean;[2] and ski resorts in Switzerland or New England; smaller towns and rural areas like the valley of the Loire River Valley in France,[3] Machu Picchu in

---

1) The **Caribbean** is a region that consists of the Caribbean Sea, its islands, and the surrounding coasts. The region is southeast of the Gulf of Mexico and the North American mainland, east of Central America, and north of South America. (excerpt from wikipedia)

2) As the term Mediterranean means" "in the middle of earth" or "between lands", it is between the continents of Africa, Asia and Europe. The Mediterranean Sea is connected to the Atlantic Ocean and to the Sea of Marmara and the Black Sea. The typical Mediterranean climate has hot, dry summers and mild, rainy winters. Crops of the region include olives, grapes, oranges, etc. With a unique combination of pleasant climate, beautiful coastline, rich history and diverse culture the Mediterranean region is the most popular tourist destination in the world—attracting approximately one third of the world's international tourists. (excerpt from wikipedia)

3) The **Loire Valley**, spanning 280 kilometers, is located in the middle stretch of the Loire River in central France. It is referred to as the *Cradle of the French* and the *Garden of France* due to the abundance of vineyards, and fruit orchards. The **Châteaux of the Loire Valley** are part of the architectural heritage of the historic towns of Amboise, Blois, and Chinon. Notable for its historic towns, architecture and wines, UNESCO added the central part of the Loire River valley to its list

Peru,[4] and the restored colonial town of Williamsburg, Virginia;[5] natural scenery like Yosemite,[6] Yellowstone;[7] Wonders of Nature like the Grand

---

of World Heritage Sites in 2000. (excerpt from wikipedia)

4) **Machu Picchu** is a 15th-century Inca site located 2,430 meters above sea level. It is situated on a mountain ridge above the Sacred Valley d in the Cusco Region, in Peru. Most archaeologists believe that Machu Picchu was built as an estate for the Inca emperor Pachacuti (1438−1472). Often referred to as the "Lost City of the Incas", it is the most familiar icon of Inca civilization. Since the site was not known to the Spanish during the colonial period, it is highly significant as a relatively intact cultural site. Machu Picchu was declared a Peruvian Historical Sanctuary in 1981 and a UNESCO World Heritage Site in 1983. In 2007, Machu Picchu was voted one of the New Seven Wonders of the World. (excerpt from wikipedia)

5) **Colonial Williamsburg** is a living-history museum. The restored Historic Area exhibits including dozens of authentic or re-created buildings related to colonial and American Revolutionary War history. Along with nearby Jamestown and Yorktown, Williamsburg forms part of the Historic Triangle. (excerpt from wikipedia)

6) **Yosemite National Park** is a United States National Park spanning eastern portions of California. Designated a World Heritage Site in 1984, Yosemite is internationally recognized for its spectacular granite cliffs, waterfalls, clear streams, giant sequoia groves, and biological diversity. Almost 95% of the park is designated wilderness. (excerpt from wikipedia)

7) **Yellowstone National Park** is a national park located primarily in the U.S. state of Wyoming, although it also extends into Montana and Idaho. Yellowstone, widely held to be the first national park in the world, is known for its wildlife and its many geothermal features, especially Old Faithful Geyser, one of the most popular features in the park. (excerpt from wikipedia)

Canyon:[8] a good bargain in Hong Kong; amusement parks in Disney enterprises.

Familiarity and boredom are the enemies of tourism. Surveys have indicated that people who spend two weeks at a resort are generally more satisfied with their holiday than those who remain three weeks or more. This means that the entire range of amusement and entertainment available is an important factor in keeping the customers satisfied. The more variety that is offered to tourists, the more pleased they will probably be.

Vocabulary

- familiarity
- amusement
- boredom
- entertainment

Comprehension

1. Each country has unique attractions. Give some examples of attractions and explain it.
2. What are the two enemies of tourism?
3. According to the survey result, what is the optimum stay in the destination?

Discussion

1. Choose one attraction and describe its main figures.

---

8) The **Grand Canyon** is a steep-sided canyon carved by the Colorado River in the state of Arizona in the United States. The Grand Canyon is 277 miles (446 km) long, up to 18 miles (29 km) wide and attains a depth of over a mile (1,800 meters). Nearly two billion years of Earth's geological history have been exposed as the Colorado River and its tributaries cut their channels through layer after layer of rock while the Colorado Plateau was uplifted. (excerpt from wikipedia)

2

Entertainment

Entertainment is a form of activity that holds the attention and interest of an audience, or gives pleasure and delight. It can be an idea or a task, but is more likely to be one of the activities or events that have developed over thousands of years specifically for the purpose of keeping an audience's attention. Although people's attention is held by different things, because individuals have different preferences in entertainment, most forms are recognizable and familiar. Entertainments initially supported by royal courts have developed into sophisticated forms and over time became available to all citizens. (en.wikipedia.org)

1. Animals

Animals have been used for the purposes of entertainment for millennia. They have been hunted for entertainment (as opposed to hunted for food); displayed while they hunt for prey; watched when they compete with each other; and watched while they perform a trained routine for human amusement. Animals that perform trained routines or "acts" for human entertainment include fleas in flea circuses,[9] dolphins in dolphinaria, and monkeys doing tricks for an audience on behalf of the player of a street organ. Animals kept in zoos in ancient times were often kept there for later use in the arena as entertainment or for their entertainment value as exotica.

The use of animals for entertainment is often controversial, especially the hunting of wild animals. Some contests between animals, once popular entertainment for the public, have become illegal because of the cruelty involved. Bullfighting, which has a strong theatrical component, is the entertainment that has a long and significant cultural history. They both involve animals and are variously regarded as sport, entertainment or cultural tradition. Among the organizations set up to advocate for the rights of animals are some whose concerns include the use of animals for entertainment. However, "in many cases of animal advocacy groups versus organizations accused of animal abuse, both sides have cultural claims."

Bullfighting[10)]

Many supporters of bullfighting regard it as a deeply ingrained, integral part of their national cultures. The aesthetic of bullfighting is based on the interaction of the man and the bull. Rather than a competitive sport, the bullfighting is more of a ritual which is judged by aficionados (bullfighting fans) based on artistic impression and command. Ernest Hemingwaysaid,"[11)] said, "Bullfighting is the only art in which the artist is in danger of death

---

9) The first people to harness fleas were watch makers who were trying to demonstrate their skills in fine manipulation. Mark Scaliot in 1578 is credited with locking a flea to a chain to display a flea pulling a chaise.

10) A 2002 Gallup poll found that 68.8% of Spaniards express "no interest" in bullfighting while 20.6% expressed "some interest" and 10.4% "a lot of interest." The poll also found significant generational variety, with 51% of those 65 and older expressing interest, compared with 23% of those between 25–34 years of age. Popularity also varies significantly according to regions in Spain with it being least popular in Galicia and Catalonia with 81% and 79% of those polled expressing no interest. Interest is greatest in the zones of the north, center, east and south, with around 37% declaring themselves fans and 63% having no interest.

11) *Death in the Afternoon* (1932)

and in which the degree of brilliance in the performance is left to the fighter's honor." Bullfighting is seen as a symbol of Spanish culture.

The bullfight is above all about the demonstration of style, technique and courage by its participants. While there is usually no doubt about the outcome, the bull is not viewed as a sacrificial victim — it is instead seen by the audience as a worthy adversary, deserving of respect in its own right. Bulls learn fast and their capacity to do so should never be underestimated. Indeed, a bullfight may be viewed as a race against time for the matador, who must display his bullfighting skills before the animal learns what is going on and begins to thrust its horns at something other than the cape. A hapless matador may find himself being pelted with seat cushions as he makes his exit.

The audience looks for the matador to display an appropriate level of style and courage and for the bull to display aggression and determination. For the matador, this means performing skillfully in front of the bull, often turning his back on it to demonstrate his mastery over the animal. The skill with which he delivers the fatal blow is another major point to look for. A skillful matador will achieve it in one stroke. Two is barely acceptable, while more than two is usually regarded as a bad job.

The moment when the matador kills the bull is the most dangerous point of the entire fight, as it requires him to reach between the horns, head on, to deliver the blow. Matadors are at the greatest risk of suffering a goring at this point. Goring is not uncommon and the results can be fatal. Many bullfighters have met their deaths on the horns of a bull.

In Spanish-speaking countries, when the bull charges through the cape, the crowd cheers saying Olé. If the matador has done exceptionally well, he will be given a standing ovation by the crowd, throwing hats and roses into the arena to show their appreciation. The successful matador will also receive one or two severed ears, and even the tail of the bull, depending on the quality of his performance. If the bull's performance was also exceptional, the public may petition the president for a vuelta(tour). This is when the crowd applauds as the dead bull is dragged once around the ring.

Despite the long history and popularity of bullfighting in Barcelona, Catalan nationalism played an important role in Barcelona's recent symbolic vote against bullfighting.[12]

Vocabulary

- millennia
- abuse
- matador
- hapless
- petition

- flea circuses
- aesthetic
- thrust
- goring

- advocacy
- adversary
- pelt
- charge

Comprehension

1. How did Ernest Hemingway mention bullfighting in his book?
2. Who is the matador? And explain his job inside the arena.
3. Explain the weapons the matador uses when he fights with a bull.
4. To the successful matador, what is given as a prize?
5. What makes bullfighting controversial?

Discussion

1. What is your opinion on bullfighting?

---

12) Bull dying in a bullfight Bullfighting is criticized by many people, including but not limited to animal rights activists, referring to it as a cruel or barbaric blood sport, in which the bull suffers severe stress and a slow, torturous death. A number of animal rights or animal welfare activist groups undertake anti-bullfighting actions in Spain and other countries.

2. Show Business

Live performances before an audience constitute a major form of entertainment, especially before the invention of audio and video recording. Performance takes a wide range of forms. Nowhere in the world is there such a vast outpouring of talent. There are more entertainer and musicians playing before live audiences in Las Vegas than in any other city in the world, and first time visitors are often surprised to find that each colorful musical production features a cast of 50 persons or more. Equally impressive are the overwhelming stage effects which combined with lavishly costumed showgirls provide show-goers with spectacles unlike any they have ever seen. And this wealth of entertainment is served up continuously every night of the week. If you miss one performance of your favorite comedian, singer or dancer there will be another show in an hour in any of the comfort lounges.

As for the big showrooms, the usual pattern is a dinner and show starting at 8 p.m., then a late beverage-only show at midnight. Some hotels offer "late-late" shows on Saturday nights beginning 2:15 a.m. Tickets are not required for Las Vegas shows. A phone call to hotel's show reservation office will insure a table reservation that evening. Naturally, as with all good show places, the early you call, the better your choice of table. But top entertainment in Las Vegas is not confined to the showrooms. To keep the fun perpetual, many hotels have theater lounges which provide a continuous stream of top name stars from dusk till dawn.

Vocabulary

- feature
- perpetual

- spectacle
- stage effect

Comprehension

1. What is the usual pattern of dinner and show?
2. Are tickets required for Las Vegas shows?

3. Theater Performance

Theatre performances, typically dramatic or musical, are presented on a stage for an audience and have a history that goes back to Hellenistic times. In the 16th and 17th centuries, European royal courts presented masks that were complex theatrical entertainments involving dancing, singing and acting. Theatre performances became "a more respectable middle-class pastime" in the late 19th and early 20th centuries, when the variety of popular entertainments increased. Operetta and music halls became available and new drama theatres such as the Moscow Art Theatre were established. Plays, musicals, monologues, and pantomimes are part of the very long history of theatre. Opera is a similarly demanding performance style that remains popular. It also encompasses all three forms, demanding a high level of musical and dramatic skill, collaboration and production expertise.

Broadway theatre, commonly called simply Broadway, is located on the side streets (between 44th and 53rd) west of Broadway, and refers to theatrical performances presented in one of the 40 large professional theaters with 500 seats or more located in the Theatre District, New York (plus one theatre in Lincoln Center) in Manhattan, New York City. Along with London's West End theatre, Broadway theatre is usually considered to represent the highest level of commercial theatre in the English-speaking world.[13]

Although there are now more exceptions than there once were, generally shows with open-ended runs operate on the same schedule, with evening performances Tuesday through Saturday with an 8 p.m. "curtain" and afternoon "matinée" performances on Wednesday, Saturday and Sunday; typically at 2 p.m. on Wednesdays and Saturdays and 3 p.m. on Sundays, making a standard eight performance a week. On this schedule, shows do not play on Monday, and the shows and theatres are said to be "dark" on that day. Actors and crew in these shows tend to regard Sunday evening

---

13) The Broadway Theatre district is a popular tourist attraction in New York City, New York. According to The Broadway League, Broadway shows sold approximately $943.3 million worth of tickets in the 2008-09 season.

through Tuesday evening as their "weekend". The Tony Award presentation ceremony is usually held on a Sunday evening in June to fit into this schedule.[14]

Vocabulary

- Monologues
- collaboration
- encompass
- pantomimes
- production expertise

Comprehension

1. Give some examples of theater performances.
2. Opera encompass three forms. Explain the three forms that compose the opera.
3. Provide some examples of theatres in the USA.
4. Explain the term "curtain" and "matinée".

Discussion

1. Find some performance theatres in Korea.

---

14) In recent years, many shows have moved their Tuesday show time an hour earlier to 7 p.m. The rationale for the move was that fewer tourists took in shows midweek, so the Tuesday crowd in particular depends on local audience members. The earlier curtain therefore allows suburban patrons time after a show to get home by a reasonable hour. Some shows, especially those produced by Disney, change their performance schedules fairly frequently, depending on the season, in order to maximize access to their targeted audience.

4. Games

Games are played for entertainment—sometimes purely for entertainment, sometimes for achievement or reward as well. They can be played alone, in teams, or online; by amateurs or by professionals. The players may have an audience of non-players, such as when people are entertained by watching a chess championship. On the other hand, players in a game may constitute their own audience as they take their turn to play. Equipment varies with the game; Board games, such as Go, Monopoly or backgammon need a board and markers; Card games, such as whist, poker and Bridge have long been played as evening entertainment among friends. For these games, all that is needed is a deck of playing cards. Other games, such as bingo, played with numerous strangers, have been organized to involve the participation of non-players via gambling. Many are geared for children, and can be played outdoors, including hopscotch, hide and seek, or Blind man's bluff. The list of ball games is quite extensive. It includes, for example, croquet, lawn bowling and paintball as well as many sports using various forms of balls. The options cater to a wide range of skill and fitness levels. Number games such as Sudoku and puzzle games like the Rubik's cube can develop mental prowess.

Video games are played using a controller to create results on a screen. They can also be played online with participants joining in remotely. In the second half of the 20th century and in the 21st century the number of such games increased enormously, providing a wide variety of entertainment to players around the world.

Vocabulary

- equipment
- constitute
- participants
- controller
- remotely

Comprehension

1. Give examples of games.
2. Give some examples of children's game.
3. On-line games are popular in the 21st century. Give some examples of it.

Discussion

1. Do you often play games? What is your favorite game?

Cultural Events

1. New Year Day

"Happy New Year!" That greeting will be said and heard for at least the first couple of weeks as a new year gets under way. But the day celebrated as New Year's Day in modern America was not always January 1.

Ancient New Years

The celebration of the New Year is the oldest of all holidays. It was first observed in ancient Babylon about 4000 years ago. In the years around 2000 BC, the Babylonian New Year began with the first New Moon (actually the first visible crescent) after the Vernal Equinox (first day of spring).[15] The beginning of spring is a logical time to start a new year. After all, it is the season of rebirth, of planting new crops, and of blossoming. January 1, on the other hand, has no astronomical nor agricultural

---

15) The Babylonian New Year celebration lasted for eleven days. Each day had its own particular mode of celebration, but it is safe to say that modern New Year's Eve festivities pale in comparison.

HAPPY NEW YEAR

significance. It is purely arbitrary.

The Romans continued to observe the New Year in late March, but their calendar was continually tampered with by various emperors so that the calendar soon became out of synchronization with the sun.

In order to set the calendar right, the Roman senate, in 153 BC, declared January 1 to be the beginning of the New Year. But tampering continued until Julius Caesar, in 46 BC, established what has come to be known as the Julian calendar. It again established January 1 as the New Year. But in order to synchronize the calendar with the sun, Caesar had to let the previous year drag on for 445 days.

The Church's View of New Year Celebrations

Although in the first centuries AD, the Romans continued celebrating the New Year, the early Catholic Church condemned the festivities as paganism. But as Christianity became more widespread, the early church began having its own religious observances concurrently with many of the pagan celebrations, and New Year's Day was no different.[16] During the middle Ages, the Church remained opposed to celebrating New Years. January 1st has been celebrated as a holiday by Western nations for only about the past 400 years.

New Year Traditions

Other traditions of the season include the making of New Year's resolutions. That tradition also dates back to the early Babylonians. Popular modern resolutions might include the promise to lose weight or quit smoking. The early Babylonian's most popular resolution was to return borrowed farm equipment.

The Rose Parade is part of "America's New Year Celebration" held in Pasadena, California each year. A festival of flower-covered floats, marching bands, equestrians and the Rose Bowl college football game on

---

16) New Years' Day is still observed as the Feast of Christ's Circumcision by some denominations.

New Year's Day was produced by the non-profit Pasadena Tournament of Roses Association. The Tournament of Roses Parade dates back to 1886. In that year, members of the Valley Hunt Club decorated their carriages with flowers. It celebrated the ripening of the orange crop in California. In 1916, the football game became a sports centerpiece of the festival.

Symbol of New Year

The tradition of using a baby to signify the New Year was begun in Greece around 600 BC. It was their tradition at that time to celebrate their god of wine, Dionysus, by parading a baby in a basket, representing the annual rebirth of that god as the spirit of fertility. Early Egyptians also used a baby as a symbol of rebirth. Although the early Christians denounced the practice as pagan, the popularity of the baby as a symbol of rebirth forced the Church to reevaluate its position. The Church finally allowed its members to celebrate the New Year with a baby, which was to symbolize the birth of the baby Jesus.

The use of an image of a baby with a New Year's banner as a symbolic representation of the New Year was brought to early America by the Germans. They had used the effigy since the fourteenth century.

For Luck in the New Year

Traditionally, it was thought that one could affect the luck they would have throughout the coming year by what they did or ate on the first day of the year. For that reason, it has become common for folks to celebrate the first few minutes of a brand new year in the company of family and friends. Parties often last into the middle of the night after the ringing in of a new year. It was once believed that the first visitor on New Year's Day would bring either good luck or bad luck the rest of the year. It was particularly lucky if that visitor happened to be a tall dark-haired man.

Traditional New Year foods are also thought to bring luck. Many cultures believe that anything in the shape of a ring is good luck, because it symbolizes "coming full

circle," completing a year's cycle. For that reason, the Dutch believe that eating donuts on New Year's Day will bring good fortune.

Many parts of the U.S. celebrate the New Year by consuming black-eyed peas. These legumes are typically accompanied by either hog jowls or ham. Black-eyed peas and other legumes have been considered good luck in many cultures. The hog, and thus its meat, is considered lucky because it symbolizes prosperity. Cabbage is another "good luck" vegetable that is consumed on New Year's Day by many. Cabbage leaves are also considered a sign of prosperity, being representative of paper currency. In some regions, rice is a lucky food that is eaten on New Year's Day.

Auld Lang Syne

The song, "Auld Lang Syne," playing in the background, is sung at the stroke of midnight in almost every English-speaking country in the world to bring in the New Year. At least partially written by Robert Burns[17] in the 1700's, it was first published in 1796 after Burns' death. Early variations of the song were sung prior to 1700 and inspired Burns to produce the modern rendition. An old Scotch tune, "Auld Lang Syne" literally means "old long ago," or simply, "the good old days." The lyrics can be found here.

(excerpted from http://adoptionworld.org/kid/newyear.html)

---

17) **Robert Burns** was a Scottish poet and lyricist. He is widely regarded as the national poet of Scotland and is celebrated worldwide. As well as making original compositions, Burns also collected folk songs from across Scotland, often revising or adapting them. His poem (and song) "Auld Lang Syne" is often sung at Hogmanay (the last day of the year), and served for a long time as an unofficial national anthem of the country. (excerpted from wikipedia)

Vocabulary

- vernal
- astronomical
- tamper
- paganism
- resolution
- reevaluate
- prosperity
- equinox
- agricultural
- synchronization
- observance
- centerpiece
- effigy
- rendition
- crescent
- arbitrary
- condemn
- denomination
- fertility
- legume

Comprehension

1. When was the New Year's Day in ancient Babylonia?
2. What changed the New Year's Day to January 1st?
3. What is the symbol of the New Year's Day?
4. What is the traditional food of the New Year's Day?
5. Explain the song "Auld Lang Syne".

Discussion

1. What is your New Year's resolution? Share it with your partner.

2. April Fool's Day

April Fools' Day, sometimes called All Fools' Day, is one of the most light-hearted days of the year. It is celebrated every year on the first day of April. Its origins are uncertain. Some see it as a celebration related to the turn of the seasons, while others believe it stems from the adoption of a new calendar. Popular since the 19th century, it is celebrated as a day when people play practical jokes and hoaxes on each other. The jokes and their victims are known as "April fools."

New Year's Day Moves

The custom of setting aside a day for the playing of harmless pranks upon one's neighbor is recognized everywhere. Some precursors of April Fools' Day include ancient cultures, e.g. the Roman festivals, which celebrated New Year's Day on or around April 1. It closely follows the vernal equinox (March 20th or March 21st). In medieval times, much of Europe celebrated March 25, the Feast of Annunciation, as the beginning of the New Year.

In 1582, Pope Gregory XIII ordered a new calendar (the Gregorian calendar) to replace the old Julian calendar. The new calendar called for New Year's Day to be celebrated Jan. 1. That year, France adopted the reformed calendar and shifted New Year's Day to Jan. 1. According to a popular explanation, many people either refused to accept the new date, or did not learn about it, and continued to celebrate New Year's Day on April 1. Other people began to make fun of these traditionalists, sending them on "fool's errands" or trying to trick them into believing something false. Eventually, the practice spread throughout Europe. In other regions such as Italy, France, etc., April 1 tradition is often known as "April fish." This includes attempting to attach a paper fish to the victim's back without being noticed. Such fish featured prominently on many late 19th- to early 20th-century French April Fools' Day postcards

Vocabulary

- adoption
- medieval
- send someone on "fool's errands

- hoax
- annunciation

- prank
- traditionalist
- prominently

Comprehension

1. The origin of April fool's day is not certain. Using the given passages, summarize its origin.
2. Explain "April fish".

Discussion

1. Give some examples of harmless pranks.

3. Buddha's Birthday

Twenty-five centuries ago, King Suddhodana ruled a land near the Himalaya Mountains. One day during a midsummer festival, his wife Queen Maya retired to her quarters to rest, and she fell asleep and dreamed a vivid dream. Four angels carried her high into White Mountain peaks and clothed her in flowers. A magnificent white bull elephant bearing a white lotus in its trunk approached Maya and walked around her three times. Then the elephant struck her on the right side with its trunk and vanished into her.

When Maya awoke, she told her husband about the dream. The King summoned 64 Brahmans to come and interpret it. Queen Maya would give birth to a son, the Brahmans said, and if the son did not leave the household, he would become a world conqueror. However, if he were to leave the household, he would become a Buddha.

When the time for the birth grew near, Queen Maya wished to travel from Kapilavatthu, the King's capital, to her childhood home, Devadaha, to give birth. With the King's blessings she left Kapilavatthu on a palanquin carried by a thousand courtiers. On the way to Devadaha, the procession passed Lumbini Grove, which was full of blossoming trees. Entranced, the Queen asked her courtiers to stop, and she left the palanquin and entered the grove. As she reached up to touch the blossoms, her son was born. Then the Queen and her son were showered with perfumed blossoms, and two streams of sparkling water poured from the sky to bathe them. And the infant stood, and took seven steps, and proclaimed "I alone am the World-Honored One!"Then Queen Maya and her son returned to Kapilavatthu. The Queen died seven days later, and the infant prince was nursed and raised by the Queen's sister Pajapati, also married to King Suddhodana.[18]

***

---

[18] Aspects of this story may have been borrowed from Hindu texts, such as the account of the birth of Indra from the Rig Veda. The story may also have Hellenic influences. For a time after Alexander the Great conquered central Asia in 334 BC, there was considerable intermingling of Buddhism with Hellenic art and ideas. There also is speculation that the story of the Buddha's birth was "improved" after Buddhist traders returned from the Middle East with stories of the birth of Jesus.

There is a jumble of symbols presented in this story. The white elephant was a sacred animal representing fertility and wisdom. The lotus is a common symbol for enlightenment in Buddhist art. A white lotus in particular represents mental and spiritual purity. The baby Buddha's seven steps evoke seven directions — north, south, east, west, up, down, and here.

In Asia, Buddha's Birthday is a festive celebration featuring parades with many flowers and floats of white elephants. Figures of the baby Buddha pointing up and down are placed in bowls, and sweet tea is poured over the figures to "wash" the baby.

Newcomers to Buddhism tend to dismiss the Buddha birth myth as so much froth. It sounds like a story about the birth of a god, and the Buddha was not a god. In particular, the declaration "I alone am the World-Honored One" is a bit hard to square with Buddhist teachings on nontheism[19] and anatman[20]. However, in Mahayana Buddhism it is said the baby Buddha was speaking of the Buddha-nature that is the immutable and eternal nature of all beings. On Buddha's birthday, some Mahayana Buddhists wish each other happy birthday, because the Buddha's birthday is everyone's birthday. Buddha's Birthday, the birthday of the Gautama Buddha traditionally celebrated in East Asia on the eighth day of the fourth month in the Chinese lunar calendar, is an official holiday in Hong Kong, Macau, and South Korea. The date varies from year to year in the Western (Gregorian) calendar:

India

The birth of the Buddha is often celebrated by Buddhists for an entire month. This month, however is not the usual Gregorian month, but rather the Month corresponding to the Buddhist calendar. The actual day is called Buddha Poornima, also traditionally known as Vaishakh Poornima. The day marks not just the birth of Shakyamuni Gautam Buddha, but also the day of Enlightenment. But as a gentle effect of West, the event of Birth is given paramount importance. The legend is that Buddha supposedly thought that

---

19) Nontheism is a term that covers a range of both religious and nonreligious attitudes characterized by the absence of or the rejection of theism or any belief in a personal god or gods.

20) In Buddhism, anattā (Pāli) or anātman (Sanskrit) refers to the notion of "not-self". One scholar describes it as "meaning non-selfhood, the absence of limiting self-identity in people and things."

asceticism[21] is the way to enlightenment, as was thought by many at that time. He sat for a prolonged time with inadequate food and water, which caused his body to shrivel so as to be indistinguishable from the bark of the tree that he was sitting under. Thinking him a sacred statue, the childless Sujata placed a bowl of kheer in front of him as an offering. Realizing that without food one can do nothing, Buddha refrained from that extreme path.

Korea

In Korea the birthday of Buddha is celebrated according to the Lunisolar calendar. This day is called 석가탄신일 (Seokga tansinil), meaning "the day of Buddha's birthday" or 부처님 오신 날 (Bucheonim osin nal) meaning "the day when Buddha arrived". Lotus lanterns cover the entire temple throughout the month which are often flooded down the street. On the day of Buddha's birth, many temples provide free meals and tea to all visitors. The breakfast and lunch provided are often sanchae bibimbap. (wikipedia)

A figure of the baby Buddha is bathed with tea.

Vocabulary

- Palanquin
- proclaim
- Asceticism

- procession
- Speculation
- Lotus lanterns

- Courtier
- immutable

---

21) Asceticism (from the Greek: ἄσκησις, áskēsis, "exercise" or "training" in the sense of athletic training) describes a lifestyle characterized by abstinence from various sorts of worldly pleasures often with the aim of pursuing religious and spiritual goals.

🎓 Comprehension

1. Find some symbols used in Buddhism.
2. When is Buddha's birthday?
3. How can you interpret the statement "I alone am the World-Honored One!"?
4. Who is Buddha?
5. How does the lotus flower symbolize Buddhism?

👥 Discussion

1. Have you ever participated in the Lotus Lantern Festival?

4. Easter: Bonnets & Bunnies

Easter (Resurrection Sunday) is a festival and holiday celebrating the Resurrection of Jesus Christ from the dead, described in the New Testament as having occurred three days after his crucifixion by Romans at Calvary. It is the culmination of events, preceded by Lent, a forty-day period of fasting, prayer, and penance. During Holy Week beginning with Palm Sunday, it reflects the return of Jesus to Jerusalem. Maundy Thursday commemorates the Last Supper of Christ and Good Friday honors the crucifixion of Jesus. Finally, Easter Sunday celebrates the resurrection after his death.

Origin: Easter, like Christmas, is a blend of paganism and Christianity. The word Easter is derived from *Eostre* (also known as *Ostara*), an ancient Anglo-Saxon Goddess. She symbolized the rebirth of the day at dawn and the rebirth of life in the spring. The arrival of spring was celebrated all over the world long before the religious meaning  became associated with Easter. Now Easter celebrates the rebirth of Christ.

Easter falls on the first Sunday on or following the spring Equinox after the full moon. The date has been calculated in this way since 325 AD. Lambs, chicks and baby creatures of all kinds are all associated with spring, symbolizing the birth of new life.

Symbols: Since ancient times many cultures have associated eggs with the universe. They've been dyed, decorated and painted by the Romans, Gaul's, Persians and the Chinese. They were used in ancient spring festivals to represent the rebirth of life. As Christianity took hold the egg began to symbolize the rebirth of man rather than nature.

Easter Egg Hunt: During the 4th century consuming eggs during Lent became taboo. However, spring is the peak egg-laying time for hens, so people began to cook eggs in their shells

to preserve them. Eventually people began decorating and hiding them for children to find during Easter, which gave birth to the Easter Egg Hunt. Other egg-related games also evolved like egg tossing and egg rolling.[22]

Easter Bunny

The Easter Bunny is a cute little rabbit that hides eggs for us to find on Easter. But where did he come from? Well, the origin is not certain. In the rites of spring the rabbit symbolized fertility. In a German book published in 1682, a tale is told of a bunny laying eggs and hiding them in the garden.

The Easter bonnet and new clothes on Easter symbolizes the end of the dreary winter and the beginning of the fresh, new spring. At the turn of the century it was popular for families to stroll to church and home again to show off their "Sunday best."

The Easter Basket shows roots in a Catholic custom. Baskets filled with breads, cheeses, hams and other foods for Easter dinner were taken to mass Easter morning to be blessed. This evolved in time to baskets filled with chocolate eggs, jellybeans, toys and stuffed bunnies for children left behind by the Easter Bunny.

Palm Sunday

In Christianity, Sunday before Easter, so called from the custom of blessing palms and of carrying portions of branches in procession, in commemoration of the triumphal entry of Jesus into Jerusalem. The custom may be traced back at least to the 4th century.

---

22) A Polish folktale tells of the Virgin Mary giving eggs to soldiers at the cross while she pleaded with them to be merciful. As her tears dropped they spattered droplets on the eggs mottling them with a myriad of colors. The Faberge egg is the best known of all the decorated eggs. Peter Faberge made intricate, delicately decorated eggs. In 1883, the Russian Czar commissioned Faberge to make a special egg for his wife.

Maundy Thursday or Holy Thursday

Thursday before Easter Sunday, observed by Christians in commemoration of Christ's Last Supper (see Eucharist). The name Maundy is derived from mandatum (Latin, "commandment").

Good Friday

Good Friday is a Christian holiday commemorating the crucifixion of Jesus Christ and his death at Calvary. It is observed during Holy Week as part of the Paschal Triduum on the Friday preceding Easter Sunday, and may coincide with the Jewish observance of Passover.

Ash Wednesday

Ash Wednesday occurs six-and-a-half weeks before Easter. In Western Christianity, the first day of the penitential season of Lent, so called from the ceremony of placing ashes on the forehead as a sign of penitence. This custom, probably introduced by Pope Gregory I, has been universal since the Synod of Benevento (1091). In the Roman Catholic Church, ashes obtained from burned palm branches of the previous Palm Sunday are blessed before mass on Ash Wednesday. The priest places the blessed ashes on the foreheads of the officiating priests, the clergy, and the congregation, while reciting over each one the following formula: "Remember that you are dust, and unto dust you shall return." (by Holly Ruggiero)

Vocabulary

• Resurrection	• culmination	• Fasting
• penance	• Commemorate	• crucifixion
• Paganism	• calculate	• Fertility
• penitence		

Comprehension

1. Explain a series of event before Easter.
2. Explain the ancient mythology related to Easter.
3. How is the Christian holiday Easter set?

4. Explain the symbols of Easter?

5. Why do we often say "Sunday best"?

Discussion

1. Share your experience in Easter with your partners.

5. Chuseok: Korean Thanksgiving Day

The 15th day of the 8th month in the lunar calendar is called Chuseok (the harvest moon) or Hangawi (the great middle of autumn) in pure Korean. Since this day marks the harvest time, it is regarded as the equivalent of American Thanksgiving Day. And it is celebrated as enthusiastically as the New Year Day. Hangawi originated from the word "Gabae". In the Silla Kingdom era, the capital was divided into six divisions. Women in the six divisions were organized into two competing groups to contest their skills in weaving hemp clothes in the presence of the king. Following the contest, they enjoyed a banquet and various pastimes. This day was called Gabae.

Nowadays, it is the second biggest holiday along with Seolnal (New Years' Day) and the celebration starts the days before Chuseok and ends with the following day. Chuseok offers a unique opportunity for family get-together to refresh the memory of our gratitude to ancestors. Early this morning, Koreans perform an ancestor worship ritual with an offer of food made of new crops, visit the tombs of their immediate ancestors and trim the plants of the tombs. Harvest crops and alcoholic beverages are attributed to the blessing of ancestors.

The Korean concept of hometown is distinct because of its affiliation with ancestor worship and its impact on the mode of observing Chuseok. The hometown is not only the place where one is born or grows up. It is also the place for enshrining the spirits of one's ancestors. Leaving one's hometown means departure from one's ancestors. This fact alone accounts for the flocking of Koreans to hometowns for reunion with relatives and the spirits of their ancestors on festive days like Chuseok and the New Year Day.

Songpyeon, a crescent-shaped rice cake, is made of rice, beans, sesame seeds, and chestnuts and is one major food prepared on Chuseok. It is steamed with pine needles to give special flavor and preservation. Every Korean cherishes childhood memories of making Songpyeon with other family members.

Chuseok is favored over other festive

days by fine weather, the full, bright moon and an abundance of foods made of new crops and various folk plays creating a festive mood. A variety of folk games are played on Chuseok, but it varies depending on locality. The most popular one is Ganggangsullae in the Cheolla Province. In the evening, children wear their traditional clothing and dance under the bright moon in a large circle. A lion dance is conducted in the north-western province, a tug of rope in the Gyeongsang Province. For all the variation of games, the farmer's musical band is prevalent in all provinces.[23]

Vocabulary

- hemp
- enshrine
- abundance
- province

- attribute
- flavor
- a tug of rope

- affiliation
- preservation
- prevalent

Comprehension

1. What does it mean by "Hangawi"?
2. What is the origin of Hangawi?
3. Explain the ancestor rituals in Korean.
4. Why do people go to their hometown? What is the special meaning of hometown?
5. Explain the traditional food and games of Hangawi.

---

23) We have taken a glimpse into the unique life patterns of Koreans through their traditional events and customs. The characteristic highlights of Koreans' life patterns are summarized as follows:

① As we appreciate in ancestor worship rituals and Seolnal's greetings, Koreans set great store in ancestor worship, filial piety to parents and respect for elders.

② There is a strong sense of community ethics that emphasizes the virtue of sharing foods and work with neighbors. Cooperative spirits are promoted through folk games played on festive days.

③ Harmony with nature is a consistent point of emphasis, as reflected in the mode of traditional costumes, the architectural design of the traditional house and the rhythm of folk plays.

④ Ancient shamanism has left its legacy in the form of belief in the supernatural power as the guardian against natural disasters. Shamanism has maintained its precarious existence amid the onslaught of modern civilization and technology.

👥 Discussion

1. The Moon has a special significance for Koreans. Exchange your ideas with your partner.
2. Compare the meaning of the Moon in the West with that of the East.

6. American Thanksgiving Day

Americans commonly trace the Thanksgiving holiday to a 1621 celebration at the
Plymouth Plantation, where the Plymouth
settlers held a harvest feast after a
successful growing season. The Pilgrims
celebrated at Plymouth for three days after
their first harvest in 1621.

The Pilgrims set ground at Plymouth Rock on December 11, 1620. Their
first winter was devastating. At the beginning of the following fall, they had
lost 46 of the original 102 who sailed on the Mayflower. But the harvest of
1621 was a bountiful one, and the remaining colonists decided to celebrate
with a feast — including 91 Indians who had helped the Pilgrims survive
their first year. It is believed that the Pilgrims would not have made it
through the year without the help of the natives. The feast was more of a
traditional English harvest festival than a true "thanksgiving" observance.

Governor William Bradford sent "four men fowling" after wild ducks
and geese. It is not certain that wild turkey was part of their feast. However,
it is certain that they had venison. The term "turkey" was used by the
Pilgrims to mean any sort of wild fowl.

Another modern staple at almost every Thanksgiving table is pumpkin
pie. But it is unlikely that the first feast included that treat. The supply of
flour had been long diminished, so there was no bread or pastries of any
kind. However, they did eat boiled pumpkin, and they produced a type of
fried bread from their corn crop. There was also no milk, cider, potatoes, or
butter. There was no domestic cattle for dairy products, and the
newly-discovered potato was still considered by many Europeans to be
poisonous. But the feast did include fish, berries, watercress, lobster, dried
fruit, clams, venison, and plums.

This "thanksgiving" feast was not repeated the following year. Many
years passed before the event was repeated. It wasn't until June of 1676 that
another Day of thanksgiving was proclaimed. On June 20 of that year the
governing council of Charlestown, Massachusetts, held a meeting to
determine how best to express thanks for the good fortune that had seen

their community securely established. By unanimous vote they instructed Edward Rawson, the clerk, to proclaim June 29 as a day of thanksgiving. It is notable that this thanksgiving celebration probably did not include the Indians, as the celebration was meant partly to be in recognition of the colonists' recent victory over the "heathen natives." (see the proclamation)

A hundred years later, in October of 1777 all 13 colonies joined in a thanksgiving celebration. It also commemorated the patriotic victory over the British at Saratoga. But it was a one-time affair.

George Washington proclaimed a National Day of Thanksgiving in 1789, although some were opposed to it. There was discord among the colonies, many feeling the hardships of a few pilgrims did not warrant a national holiday. And later, President Thomas Jefferson opposed the idea of having a day of thanksgiving.

It was Sarah Josepha Hale, a magazine editor, whose efforts eventually led to what we recognize as Thanksgiving. Hale wrote many editorials championing her cause in her Boston Ladies' Magazine, and later, in Godey's Lady's Book. Finally, after a 40-year campaign of writing editorials and letters to governors and presidents, Hale's obsession became a reality when, in 1863, President Lincoln proclaimed the last Thursday in November as a national day of Thanksgiving.

Thanksgiving was proclaimed by every president after Lincoln. The date was changed a couple of times, most recently by Franklin Roosevelt, who set it up one week to the next-to-last Thursday in

order to create a longer Christmas shopping season. Public uproar against this decision caused the president to move Thanksgiving back to its original date two years later. And in 1941, Thanksgiving was finally sanctioned by Congress as a legal holiday, as the fourth Thursday in November. (http://wilstar.com/holidays/thankstr.htm)

🗂 Vocabulary

- devastating
- poisonous
- patriotic
- venison
- unanimous
- proclaim
- fowl
- heathen

🎓 Comprehension

1. Who is it that claimed a National Day of Thanksgiving?
2. What is the traditional food of Thanksgiving?
3. When is the date of Thanksgiving?

👥 Discussion

1. Summarize the history of Pilgrims' settlement in America.
2. Compare Korean Thanksgiving day with American Thanksgiving, and discuss the differences and similarities.

7. Halloween

Halloween (a contraction of "All Hallows' Evening") is a yearly celebration observed in a number of countries on 31 October. Typical festive Halloween activities include trick-or-treating, attending costume parties, decorating, carving pumpkins into jack-o'-lanterns.

The First Halloween

Hundreds of years before the birth of Christ, the Celts—the inhabitants of parts of France and the British Isles—held a festival at the beginning of every winter for the Lord of the Dead. The Celts believed that this god ruled the world in winter, when he called together the ghosts of dead people. On October 31, people believed these spirits of the dead came back to earth in the forms of animals. They thought that very bad ghosts came back as black cats. At their festival on this day, the Celts used to make big fires to frighten the ghosts and chase them away. This celebration was the beginning of the holiday of Halloween.

The Origin Halloween Customs

The Romans, who ruled the British Isles after the birth of Christ, also held a celebration at the beginning of winter. Because this was harvest time, the Romans brought apples and nuts for the goddess of gardens. Later, the Christians added their customs to those of the Celts and the Romans. They had a religious holiday on November 1 for the saints (the unusually good people in Christianity), which they called All Hallows' or All Saints' Day. The evening before this day was All Hallows' Even ("holy evening"); later the name became Halloween.

Witches: A Symbol of Halloween

Long ago in Britain, people used to go to wise old women called "witches" to learn about the future. They believed that these witches had the power to tell the future and to sue magic words to protect people or change them. There were many beliefs about witches, who are now a symbol of Halloween. For example, people believed witches flew on broomsticks to big, secret meetings, where they ate, sang, and danced. The Christians tried to stop people from believing in witches, but many uneducated people, especially in the countryside, held on to their beliefs.

Halloween Today

When people came to North America from the British Isles, they brought their Halloween customs with them. Today, Halloween is a night when children dress up like ghosts, witches, devils, and so on. They go from house to house in their costumes, ring doorbells, and shout, "Trick or treat!" People give them candy, apples, gum, and nuts, and the children have a good time. But most children have no idea that their holiday has such a long history.

Vocabulary

- Inhabitant
- Trick or treat
- Celt
- costume parties
- Witch
- jack-o'-lanterns

Comprehension

1. What is the origin of Halloween?
2. Who firstly celebrated the October 31st festival?
3. How does the Roman festival relate to present Halloween celebration?
4. Why did witches become a symbol of Halloween?
5. What is today's Halloween?

Discussion

1. Summarize the Celt's October festival, and associate it with the Halloween tradition.

8. Christmas

Christmas (meaning "Christ's Mass") is an annual festival commemorating the birth of Jesus Christ, observed generally on December 25 as a religious and cultural celebration among billions of people around the world. Christmas is a holiday shared and celebrated by many religions. It is a day that has an effect on the entire world. To many people, it is a favorite time of the year involving

gift giving, parties and feasting. Christmas is a holiday that unifies almost all of professing Christendom. The spirit of Christmas causes people to decorate their homes and churches, cut down trees and bring them into their homes, decking them with silver and gold. In the light of that tree, families make merry and give gifts one to another.

When the sun goes down on December 24th, and darkness covers the land, families and churches prepare for participation in customs such as burning the yule log, singing around the decorated tree, kissing under the mistletoe and holly, and attending a late night service or midnight mass.

Origin of Christmas

The date of December 25th comes from Rome and was a celebration of the Italic god, Saturn, and the rebirth of the sun god. It was noted by the pre-Christian Romans and other pagans, that daylight began to increase after December 22nd, when they assumed that the sun god died. These ancients believed that the sun god rose from the dead three days later as the new-born and venerable sun.

This was a cause for much wild excitement and celebration. Gift giving and merriment filled the temples of ancient Rome, as sacred priests of Saturn, called dendrophori, carried wreaths of evergreen boughs in procession.

In Germany, the evergreen tree was used in worship and celebration of the yule god, also in observance of the resurrected sun god. The evergreen

tree was a symbol of the essence of life and was regarded as a phallic symbol in fertility worship. Witches and other pagans regarded the red holly as a symbol of the menstrual blood of the queen of heaven, also known as Diana. The white berries of mistletoe were believed by pagans to represent droplets of the semen of the sun god. Both holly and mistletoe were hung in doorways of temples and homes to invoke powers of fertility in those who stood beneath and kissed, causing the spirits of the god and goddess to enter them. These customs transcended the borders of Rome and Germany to the far reaches of the known world.

The word "Christmas"

The word "Christmas" is a combination of the words "Christ" and "Mass". The word "Mass" means death and was coined originally by the Roman Catholic Church, and belongs exclusively to the Church of Rome. The ritual of the Mass involves the death of Christ, and Christmas is strictly a Roman Catholic word.

In England, as the authorized Bible became available to the common people by the decree of King James the II in 1611, people began to discover the pagan roots of Christmas, which are clearly revealed in Scripture. The Puritans in England, and later in Massachusetts Colony, outlawed this holiday as witchcraft. Near the end of the nineteenth century, when other Bible versions began to appear, there was a revival of the celebration of Christmas.

(excerpted from Lawrence Kelemen)

Vocabulary

- yule log
- wreath
- decree
- mistletoe
- holly
- revival
- venerable
- transcend

🎓 Comprehension

1. Summarize the Christian holiday Christmas.
2. Give some examples of Christmas symbols, and explain their meaning.
3. Discuss the spirit of Christmas.

👥 Discussion

1. Think of Christmas presents you can prepare for your family and friends.

VII
PART

Perspectives in Tourism

1

Specialty Travel Forms of Tourism

Specialty travel forms of tourism have emerged over the years, each with its own adjective. Many of these have come into common use by the tourism industry and academics.

1. Sustainable Tourism

"Sustainable tourism is envisaged as leading to management of all resources in such a way that economic, social and aesthetic needs can be fulfilled while maintaining cultural integrity, essential ecological processes, biological diversity and life support systems." (World Tourism Organization)

2. Ecotourism

"Tourism involving travel to areas of natural or ecological interest, typically under the guidance of a naturalist, for the purpose of observing wildlife and learning about the environment and at the same time focus on wildlife and promotion of understanding and conservation of the

environment." (http://www.ecoindia.com)

This is a conscientious form of tourism and tourism development, which encourages going back to natural products in every aspect of life and helps preserve nature. It is also the key to sustainable ecological development. [1]

3. Medical Tourism

When there is a significant price difference between countries for a given medical procedure, particularly in Southeast Asia, India, Eastern Europe and where there are different regulatory regimes, in relation to particular medical procedures (e.g. dentistry), traveling to take advantage of the price or regulatory differences is often referred to as medical tourism.[2]

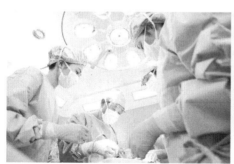 

---

1) Ecotourism, also known as ecological tourism, is responsible travel to fragile, pristine, and usually protected areas that strives to be low impact and (often) small scale.

2) Korean government has interested on the medical tourism since 2007.

4. Educational Tourism

With growing popularity of teaching and learning, and enhancing technical competency outside of the classroom environment, educational tourism developed. In educational tourism, the main focus of the tour or leisure activity includes visiting another country to learn about the culture, such as in Student Exchange Programs and Study Tours, or to work and apply skills acquired inside the classroom in a different environment, such as in the International Practicum Training Program.

5. Culture Tourism

From the early seventeenth century, a new form of tourism developed as a direct outcome of the freedom and quest for learning heralded by the Renaissance. It became customary for the education of a gentleman to be completed by a "Grand tour" of major cultural centers of Europe, accompanied by a tutor and often-lasting three years or more. Paris, Venice, or Florence was the destination to enjoy the rival cultures and social life. By the end of the eighteenth century, the custom had become institutionalized for the gentry. As a form of cultural tourism, creative tourism has existed. Creative tourism is defined as tourism related to the active participation of travellers in the culture of the host community, through interactive workshops and informal learning experiences.

2

Nature in Tourism

1. The Role of Nature in the Holiday Experience

The role that nature plays in the holiday experience is difficult to define, but it plays a very diverse role. It can:

Enhance the experience – meaning the natural environment forms a picturesque and relaxing backdrop to a particular activity. It adds to the emotional connection a visitor forms with a destination or experience.

Be crucial to the experience – meaning the holiday activity would not exist or would be severely compromised without nature. This type of holiday experience is about being immersed in, and surrounded by, nature.

2. The Ideal Nature Holiday

The ideal nature-based holiday is:
- A place with bushland and water (preferably a beach).
- Relatively unspoilt and not overdeveloped.
- A location with enough people around for security, but not over-crowded.
- Quiet with fresh air.
- A location with some comforts within easy reach –that is, has well equipped and comfortable accommodation.
- A location with a town nearby with provisions, cafes, restaurant, crafts/antique shops.
- A place with lots of things to do whether sedentary and observational (such as enjoying the view or lazing on the beach) or more active (such as bushwalking, fishing, swimming).

3. Appeal To The Senses

The research also showed that visitors want to connect with nature using all their senses. They want to experience a heightened sensory awareness that may be missing in their everyday existence. They want their getaway to provide them with
opportunities to:
- **Feel** the sand between their toes.
- **Look** at the beautiful landscape.
- **Taste** the salt air.
- **Hear** the animals, birds, or nothing at all (and appreciate the quietness).
- **Smell** the flora and fresh air.

4. Dare To Be Different

Just as nature provides a range of experiences, opportunities and marvels, so too should tourism operators. The research showed that visitors don't want the same nature-based holiday wherever they go. They want to experience something different, something out of the ordinary, and something which prompts an emotional reaction. They want to experience something special which will turn their short-break away into a lifelong memory.

Dare to be different. Dare to provide your visitors with a unique activity or physical setting which capitalizes on and enhances your natural surrounds. In the eyes of your visitors, this will set you apart from the rest.

(www.sydneyaustralia.com)

3

Careers in Tourism

Job Forecasts

The World Travel and Tourism Council (WTTC) estimates that today there are 231 million people worldwide, some 10 percent of the total workforce, employed in jobs that exist because of the demand generated by tourism. While tourism contributes to gross domestic product (GDP), capital investment, employment, foreign exchange, and export earnings, it is the job creation capacity of tourism that is its most significant feature. By 2010, WTTC forecasts that there will be 328 million people around the globe having jobs created by tourism.

Job Requirements

Are you suited to work in the tourism field? Do you like working with people? Would you be genuinely concerned for a customer's comfort, needs, and well-being even if the customer might be rude and obnoxious? If you can answer in the affirmative, you can find a place in this industry. You have to like to do things for other people and work helpfully with them. If not, this is not the industry for you. Courtesy comes easily when customers are pleasant and gracious. But a great deal of self-discipline is required to serve every type of person—especially demanding and indecisive ones. In tourism, the customer might often change his or her mind. This requires patience and an unfailing cheerful personality.

You must also ask if you have the physical stamina required to carry out many of the jobs available. It is difficult to work long hours on your feet or to work in a hot, humid, or cold environment. You might be involved in the pressure of a crush of people, such as at an airline ticket counter. A travel agency counselor must have keen vision, excellent hearing, and well-endowed nerves. Try to evaluate your physical attributes and skills to determine if you can perform.

To enhance your chances of getting a job and deciding if you would like it, visit several types of tourist-related organizations. Watch the activities being performed. Talk to managers, supervisors, and employees. Try to obtain an internship. Work experience means a great deal. Once you have had that, these skills can be utilized in a wide variety of tourism enterprises in any number of locations.

Career Opportunity

Like most service industries, tourism is labor-intensive; that is, it employs a high proportion of people in comparison to the number that it serves. The range of jobs is also very wide, from unskilled, like a dishwasher in a restaurant, to semi-skilled, like a waiter or a chambermaid, to skilled, like a travel agent or a statistician. In addition, tourism generates many jobs that are not usually considered to be within the industry itself—jobs in construction, manufacturing, and merchandising.

We have stressed throughout our discussion that tourism is not a single industry, but rather a group of related enterprises that are joined together in the common purpose of providing services for the traveling public. Among them are the transportation companies—air, rail, ship, and bus; the accommodations companies—hotels, motels, camping grounds, and marinas; catering services—restaurants, bars, night clubs, and food stores; and the wide variety of stores and entertainment that contributes to the amusement of the tourist. In other books in this series, there are detailed discussions of careers in the airlines, in the merchant marine, in hotels, and in restaurants. Here, we will discuss the positions that pull the entire field of tourism together into a single entity—travel agents, tour operators, guides, and so on.

A majority of the jobs in tourism, regardless of which part of the industry they concern, have one common denominator: **contact with the public**, including both the positive and negative aspects of dealing with ordinary human beings. We have pointed out that openly expressed resentment of tourists has caused a decline in business in some resort areas. Anyone who has chosen a career in tourism should enjoy working with people and be tolerant of their failings, especially since the irritations of travel can bring out the worst qualities in some people.

In many of the jobs in which it is necessary to deal with the public, language skill is necessary or desirable. People who hold jobs of this kind include travel agency employees, ticket and reservations agents, airline flight personnel, front-desk employees in hotels, tour conductors or guides, waiters, barmen, and so forth. The degree of language skill may vary, from using special terms in catering service jobs to speaking fluently among travel agents and tour guides. The degree of language skill may also vary according to the location of the job. Greater skill is required in tourist destination areas than in market areas. In the latter, travel personnel usually work with their own nationals. However, there is not always a clear distinction between a destination and a market area. Paris is an excellent case in point, since it both receives and generates large numbers of tourists.

The tourist industry differs from many others in that it employs more women than many other kinds of business. Indeed, women are found at all levels—from the semi-skilled to management positions—in the transportation companies. Many successful travel agents are women who have established independent enterprises after gaining experience elsewhere in the industry.

Experience is necessary for the successful operation of a travel agency. It has been estimated that a minimum of ten years' work in the industry is a prerequisite for setting up an agency with the expectation of making it a success. There are many different ways to acquire the necessary experience. Some agents begin as clerical workers or secretaries in travel agencies or in the transportation companies. Particular jobs that provide useful knowledge include those of ticket agent and reservations agent for the airlines.

In addition to dealing with the public, the travel agent must deal with people who work for the other components in the industry. One of the most important aspects of the job is keeping informed of the highly complex pricing policies of both scheduled and nonscheduled airlines, and the resort hotels as well. Even when help is available, as it usually is from the airlines, the agent who can compute fares accurately has an advantage over one who cannot. The agent must also keep up with other developments in the industry—new resorts, changing travel regulations, new services, and so on.

We have already touched on some of the advantages **the travel agent** has. One of the most important is the economic independence that comes from owning and operating a small business. There is of course an element of risk. A change in the business cycle as a whole may cause a sharp decline in tourism, which is after all a luxury for most people. Another advantage that we have mentioned is the opportunity to travel. The treatment that is given to travel agents on familiarization tours is often lavish so as to impress them favorably with the services that are being offered.

The people who write about travel also receive lavish treatment from the tourist industry. There are relatively few travel writers, but they fill an important place in publicizing the industry. Some of them work full-time for magazines or newspapers. Others are **free-lancers**; that is, they work for themselves and sell their articles to any publication that is interested in them. There is also a small industry involved in writing and publishing travel guidebooks. Some of these, like the Baedeker guides that were very popular in the 19th Century and the Michelin guides that have wide circulation today, are sold all over the world. The Michelin series, incidentally, is essentially a public relations effort on the part of the French automobile tire manufacturer. Travel writing appeals to people who have a talent with words and who like both travel and independence.

The tour operators work much more within the framework of ordinary corporate practice than the small retail agencies do. That is, they have the usual hierarchy of clerical workers and management personnel. Companies like Cook and American Express employ people in nearly all phases of tourism, ranging from the jobs that would be found in a retail travel agency to those that deal with packaging tours or establishing overall policy for the companies. They also employ a large staff to work on advertising and publicity. The large companies are an excellent place to gain experience. People often start with clerical work and later move on to more travel-oriented jobs.

Official and semi-official tourist bureaus also employ many people who perform different kinds of work. Some of the jobs—including both advertising and publicity—are related to promotion, which is extremely important to the whole industry. Others are involved with research, such as gathering travel statistics and trying to work out systems that increase their accuracy. Still others are concerned with planning and development of new tourist facilities, or with the maintenance and improvement of existing facilities. The heads of the government bureaus may control official policy concerning tourism within an entire country or region. This may be important enough to the government so that the top official holds the rank of cabinet minister. A great deal of the work in government tourist bureaus involves contact primarily with people in other aspects of the industry, but some may have direct contact with the public in giving information or in solving complaints or problems for tourists.

Consulting firms also play a part in the tourist industry. A consultant offers the expertise he has acquired through study and experience to individual clients on a fee basis. In tourism, consultants are called in to give advice to government tourist bureaus or private developers. Some of them may perform market research; some may analyze statistics that have been collected; and some may help in the planning of new resorts.

Perhaps the most distinctive and difficult job in the entire industry belongs to the tour guide or conductor. There are in fact two types of **tour guides**, one in charge of local sightseeing, and the other accompanying a group throughout its travels and making all the arrangements for the group. The term guide is often used for the first of these jobs and **conductor** for the second. The sightseeing guide must of course be familiar with the points of interest that he is showing to the visitors. He usually gives a prepared talk that describes the points of interest, but he must also be prepared to answer a lot of questions. And of course he has to deal with any problems that occur during the tour or excursion. These may include bad weather, sudden illness, an accident—it would be impossible to name everything that might happen. A sightseeing guide needs two qualities above all-an outgoing personality and language skill.

The guide or conductor who stays with a group throughout its trip needs these same two qualities. He also needs to have a through knowledge of the workings of all kinds of transportation systems and of the regulations and red tape that the tourists will meet when going from one country to another.

One of his jobs involves handling the baggage for his group; another concerns easing them through government formalities; and yet another involves making sure they get the kind of accommodations, food, and entertainment they have paid for. These are the aspects of travel that are likely to cause the most problems and create the most irritation when they go wrong. The guide often has to display the qualities of a diplomat, not only in dealing with the tourists themselves, but also with all the officials, baggage handlers, hotel clerks, and the many other people who are constant figures on the travel scene.

Another distinctive job in tourism is that of **social director**. Many resort hotels and nearly all cruise ships employ a person who is in charge of the activities that are supposed to entertain and amuse the customers. The social director not only has to organize these activities, he must also involve the willing and the reluctant guests in the fun and games. An extroverted person is essential to a job of this kind; a good social director should really enjoy the games and parties that are planned for the guests. In addition to social directors, resorts employ people to supervise activities in which the resorts specialize—golf and tennis pros, or swimming, skiing, and scuba diving instructors. These people, like entertainers, have talents acquired outside the field of tourism, yet their employment in resorts indicates the wide range of occupations that draw on tourism for economic support.

We have frequently mentioned experience in this discussion of careers in the tourist industry. In addition, there are many facilities for formal training for several types of jobs in the industry. The airlines, for example, have training programs for ticket and reservations agents and flight attendants. Many hotel companies also give training courses to people who will fill both skilled and semi-skilled positions. In some cases, governments have stepped in to operate schools to turn out people who can fill jobs in the hotel and catering industries. This is often an important part of planning the development of new tourist industries. The willingness of governments to open such schools often acts as an incentive for private investors to settle on a particular area. Commercial schools also provide training for prospective airline personnel or for people who wish to go into the hotel or restaurant businesses. In these schools, the individuals who are interested in the work pay for the training themselves.

A few universities, especially in the United States and the United Kingdom, have also begun to offer courses in tourism as a whole. People who get a university degree after completing such a curriculum can be considered professionals in the field. They are particularly well-qualified to fill positions with government tourist bureaus or with consulting firms. Their education is designed to give an overview of all aspects of the industry. It is particularly useful in research, planning, and development.

Tourism is an industry that is still growing rapidly. It continues to provide people with the choice of a variety of occupations that require many different kinds of skills. No matter what aspect of the industry one may work in, the final result of the effort should be a satisfied customer who remembers his trip or his vacation with pleasure.

Career Possibilities

Tourism today is one of the world's largest industries. It is made up of many segments, the principal ones being transportation, accommodations, food service, shopping, travel arrangement, and activities for tourists, such as history, culture, adventure, sports, recreation, entertainment, and other similar activities. The businesses that provide these services require knowledgeable business managers.

Familiarity with tourism, recreation, business, and leisure equips one to pursue a career in a number of tourism-related fields. Even during times of severe economic downturn, tourism has performed well. Tourism skills are critically needed, and there are many opportunities available in a multitude of fields.

Because tourism is diverse and complex and each sector has many job opportunities and **career paths**, it is virtually impossible to list and describe all the jobs one might consider in this large field. However, as a student interested in tourism, you could examine the following areas, many of which are discussed in more detail in Chapters 5 to 8.

Airlines

The airlines are a major travel industry employer, offering a host of jobs at many levels, ranging from entry level to top management. Illustrative jobs are reservation agents, flight attendants, pilots, flight engineers, aircraft mechanics, maintenance staff, baggage handlers, airline food service jobs, sales representatives, sales jobs, computer specialists, training staff, office jobs, clerical positions, ticket agents, and research jobs. Because airlines have to meet safety and other requirements, opportunities also exist with the Federal Aviation Adminstration (FAA). The FAA hires air traffic controllers and various other specialists. Airports also use a wide range of personnel from parking attendants to managers. Other air-related jobs are available with associations such as the Air Transport Association.

Bus Companies

Bus companies require management personnel, ticket agents, sales representatives, tour representatives, hostesses, information clerks, clerical positions, bus drivers, personnel people, and training employees.

Cruise Companies

The cruise industry is the fastest-growing segment of the tourism industry today. Job opportunities include those for sales representatives, clerical workers, market researchers, and recreation directors. Because of its similarity in operations, the cruise industry has many of the same jobs as the lodging industry.

Railroads

Passenger rail service is currently dominated by Amtrak, which hires passenger service representatives, sales representatives, reservation clerks and other types of clerks, conductors, engineers, coach and lounge car attendants, and station agents.

Rental Car Companies

With increased pleasure air travel and the growth of fly/drive programs, rental car companies are becoming an even more important segment of the travel industry. This sector of tourism employs reservation agents, rental sales agents, clerks of various kinds, service agents, mechanics, and district and regional managers.

Hotels, Motels, and Resorts

The range of jobs in hotels and motels is extremely broad. The following list is representative: general manager, resident manager, comptroller, accountants, management trainees, director of sales, director of convention sales, director of personnel, director of research, mail clerks, room clerks, reservation clerks, front office manager, housekeepers, superintendent of service, bellhops, lobby porters, doormen, maids, chefs, cooks, kitchen helpers, storeroom employees, dishwashers, waiters, bartenders, apprentice waiters, heating and air conditioning personnel, maintenance workers, engineers, electricians, plumbers, carpenters, painters, and laundry workers.

Resorts tend to have the same jobs as those mentioned for hotels and motels; however, larger resorts will have greater job opportunities and require more assistants in all areas. Resorts also have a number of additional job opportunities in the areas of social events, entertainment, and recreation, such as for tennis and golf pros. At ski resorts there will be ski instructors, members of a safety patrol, and so on. The American Hotel and Motel Association estimates that the lodging industry employs approximately 1.64 million people; and by the year 2005, lodging industry labor demands will increase 25 percent.

Travel Agencies

Travel agencies range from very small to very large businesses. The smaller businesses are very much like any other small business. Very few people carry out all the business operations, and jobs include secretarial, travel counseling, and managerial activities. In large offices, job opportunities are more varied and include commercial account specialists, domestic travel counselors, international travel counselors, research directors, and advertising managers. Trainee group sales consultants, accountants, file clerks, sales personnel, tour planners, tour guides, reservationists, group coordinators, trainees, operations employees, administrative assistants, advertising specialists, and computer specialists are other possibilities.

Tour Companies

Tour companies offer employment opportunities in such positions as tour manager or escort, tour coordinator, tour planner, publicist, reservations specialist, accountant, sales representative, group tour specialist, incentive tour coordinator, costing specialist, hotel coordinator, office supervisor, and managerial positions. Often, a graduate will begin employment as a management trainee, working in all the departments of the company before a permanent assignment is made.

Food Service

Many job opportunities are available in the rapidly growing food service industry, such as head waiters, captains, waiters, waitresses, bus persons, chefs, cooks, bartenders, restaurant managers, assistant managers, personnel directors, dieticians, menu planners, cashiers, food service supervisors, purchasing agents, butchers, beverage workers, hostesses, kitchen helpers, and dishwashers.

Tourism Education

As tourism continues to grow, the need for training and education grows. In recent years many colleges and universities have added travel and tourism programs, existing programs have expanded, vocational schools have launched programs, trade associations have introduced education and certification programs, and private firms have opened travel schools. There are job opportunities for administrators, teachers, professors, researchers, and support staff.

Tourism Research

Tourism research consists of the collection and analysis of data from both primary and secondary sources. The tourism researcher plans market studies, consumer surveys, and the implementation of research projects. Research jobs are available in tourism with airlines, cruise lines, management consulting firms, state travel offices, and so on.

Travel Communications

There are a number of opportunities available in travel writing as editors, staff writers, and freelance writers. Most major travel firms have a need for public relations people who write and edit, disseminate information, develop communication vehicles, obtain publicity, arrange special events, do public speaking, plan public relations campaigns, and so on. A travel photographer could find employment in either public relations or travel writing. Television is a medium with increasing opportunities.

Recreation and Leisure

Jobs in recreation and leisure are enormous. Some examples are activity director, aquatics specialist, ski instructor, park ranger, naturalist, museum guide, handicapped program planner, forester, camping director, concert promoter, lifeguards, tennis and golf instructors, coaches for various athletic teams, and drama directors. Many recreation workers teach handicrafts. Resorts, parks, and recreation departments often employ recreation directors who hire specialists to work with senior citizens or youth groups, to serve as camp counselors, or to teach such skills as boating and sailing. Management, supervisory, and administrative positions are also available.

Attractions

Attractions such as amusement parks and theme parks are a major source of tourism employment. Large organizations such as Disney World, Disneyland, Six Flags, Worlds of Fun, and Sea World provide job opportunities ranging from top management jobs to clerical and maintenance jobs.

Festivals and Events

Festivals and events are one of the fastest growing segments of the tourism industry. Event management is emerging as a field, is becoming more professional, and is providing a new source of job opportunities. Events are creating offices and moving them to year-round operation. A study of the International Special Events Society showed that event managers earned between $25,000 and $75,000 per year and that the majority held baccalaureate degrees.

Sports Tourism

Sports are popular throughout the world, with many sports teams and enterprises becoming big businesses offering job opportunities in the management and marketing areas.

Tourist Offices and Information Centers

Numerous jobs are available in tourist offices and information centers. Many chambers of commerce function as information centers and hire employees to provide this information. Many states operate welcome centers.

Job titles found in state tourism offices are: director, assistant director, deputy director, travel representative, economic development specialist, assistant director for travel promotion, statistical analyst, pubic information officer, assistant director for public relations, marketing coordinator, communications specialist, travel editor, media liaison, media specialist, photographer, administrative assistant, information specialist, media coordinator, manager of travel literature, writer, chief of news and information, marketing coordinator, market analyst, research analyst, economist, reference coordinator, secretary, package tour coordinator, and information clerk.

Convention and Visitors Bureaus

As more and more cities enter the convention and visitor industry, employment opportunities in this segment grow. Many cities are devoting public funds to build convention centers to compete in this growing market. Convention and visitors bureaus require managers, assistant managers, research directors, information specialists, marketing managers, public relations staff, sales personnel, secretaries, and clerks.

Meeting Planners

A growing profession is meeting planning. Many associations and corporations are hiring people whose job responsibilities are to arrange, plan, and conduct meetings.

Gaming

One of the fastest-growing sectors is gaming. Today, one is hard-pressed to find a state where gambling is not allowed or a gaming proposal is in front of the state legislature. From riverboats to Indian reservations to land-based casinos, new destinations are being created. Casinos provide job opportunities ranging from managers to marketers to mechanics to clerical and maintenance jobs.

Other Opportunities

A fairly comprehensive list of career opportunities has been presented. Others that do not fit the general categories listed are club management, corporate travel departments, hotel representative companies, in-flight and trade magazines, and trade and professional associations.

Vocabulary

- statistician
- airline agent
- free-lancers
- conductor
- government tourist bureau
- denominator
- publicizing
- cabinet minister
- red tape
- ticket agent
- lavish
- consultant
- social director

Comprehension

1. What could be the requirements to work in the tourism industry?
2. What is the common denominator of a majority of the jobs in tourism?
3. Describe the jobs in which language skills are desirable or necessary?
4. What positions do women frequently hold in the tourist industry?
5. What could be the most important advantages in becoming a travel agent?
6. How can writers be involved in the travel and tourist business?
7. Explain the job responsibilities of a tour guide or conductor who stays with a group?
8. Why do we often say that the tour conductor should have the qualities of a diplomat?
9. What sort of person makes a good social director?
10. Give some examples of the trainings that are offered by companies within the tourist industry.

APPENDIX

GLOSSARY

CT100

Accommodations	hotels or other places where a traveler can find rest and shelter
Attraction	a place, event, building or area which tourists want to visit
Affinity Groups	groups traveling to the same place for a similar purpose
Biodiversity	a variety of wildlife in an area
Business plan	an action plan that entrepreneurs draw up for the purpose of starting a business; a guide to running one's business
Caravaning	Cars equipped with sleeping quarters and even stoves and refrigerators
Catering Facilities	places where a traveler or another member of the public can find food and drink.
Component	a constituent part
Culture	people's customs, clothing, food, houses, language, dancing, music, drama, literature and religion
CIT	charter inclusive tour, one that utilizes a charter airplane for transportation.
Cruise	a voyage by ship
Destination	the end point of a journey

Diversity	variety; multiplicity; range; assortment
Disposable income	income above and beyond what is needed for basic expenses such as food, shelter, clothing, and taxes
Domestic	within one's own country. A domestic tourist is a person who engages in tourism in his/her own country; domestic flights are those within the airline's own country.
Economy	wealth of resources of a community
Ecosystem	an area where living and non-living things interact
Eco-tourism	a combination of tourism and the environment (e.g. planning before development; sustainability of resources; economic viability of a tourism product; no negative impact on either the environment or local communities; responsibility for the environment from developers, the tourism industry and tourists; environmentally-friendly practices by all parties concerned and economic benefits flowing to local communities)
Endangered species	in severe danger of becoming extinct in the near future unless immediate steps are taken to protect the species
Environment	the diverse community activities and cultures of a country's inhabitants, as well as its scarce and sensitive natural resources
Event	an occurrence of importance
Excursionist	a person who is away from his usual residence for less than 24 hours, or at most a weekend
Fauna	all the animals of a particular area
Flora	all the plants of a particular area
Franchise	The hotel and its operation are designed by the corporation, but the right to run it is sold or leased
Gateway	the point of access to a country or region, usually an airport or seaport, although certain frontier points and railway stations can be given the designation
Global	worldwide
Guest House	one or two rooms
Heritage	a very broad expression that describes anything that has a link with some past event or person (e.g. cultural heritage refers to past customs and

	traditions with the unspoken implication that these are worthwhile or creditable)
Heritage site	a place that capitalises on its connection with heritage
Human-made attraction	an attraction created by people
Icon	a symbol representing something
Inbound tourist	tourist coming into a country from another country
Incentive Trip	A bonus or reward
International Tourism	the travel of tourists from one country to another
Internal or Domestic Tourism	travel within only one country
Itinerary	the written details of a customer's travel arrangements in the form of dates, times and destinations
IT	inclusive tour, a travel package that offers both transportation and accommodations, and often entertainment as well.
ITX	tour-basing fares.
Labor-intensive	a large number of workers in proportion to the people who are served.
Leakage	the money that goes out of the economy
Load Factor	the percentage of seats that have been sold on a flight
Local	belonging to a particular place or region
Marina	boats for accommodations and transportation
Motel	made up from motor and hotel
Multiplier effect	Money paid for wages or in other ways is spent not once but sometimes several times for other items in the economy
Natural attraction	a tourist attraction that has not been made or created by people
Occupancy Rate	percentage of rooms or beds that are occupied
Outbound tourist	a tourist departing to a destination beyond the borders of the country of residence
Package Tour	refers to a set of products and services offered to the visitors that is composed of varieties of tourism characteristic products (such as transport, accommodation, food services, recreation, etc.). The component of a package tour might be pre-established, or can result from an "a la carte" procedure where the visitor decides the combination of products/services he/she wishes to acquire.

	This can be synonymously used with "package travel and/or package holiday".
Pension	a small establishment with perhaps ten to twenty guest rooms
Price elastic market	respond to lower fares and other inducements in pricing, in selecting the destination
Profitability	capacity to make profit
Region	an area of land having more or less definable boundaries
Resident	An institutional unit is resident in a country when it has a center of economic interest in the economic territory of that country.
Retail Travel Agents	sell the tours directly to the public through their own travel offices and through other agents
Scheduled Airline	operate on fixed routes at fixed times according to a timetable
Self-Contained Resort Complex	consists of a hotel and recreational facilities
Service	work done for the benefit of another
Service delivery	the manner in which customer needs are met
Service provider	a person or company that supplies a particular service
Souvenir	a product purchased by a tourist as a reminder of a holiday
Sustainable	something which can be kept in the same or a better condition for the future
Tour	refers to any arranged journey intended for purposes of tourism to one or more places and back to the point of origin. The arranged journey may not necessarily be pre-paid.
Tour Guide	pertains to an individual who guides visitors for a fee, commission, or any form of lawful remuneration or a personnel from a government or private entity who performs the above function without fee or remuneration.
Tour Operator	refers to entities engaged in the business of extending/selling travel services (e.g., arrangements and bookings for transportation and/or accommodation; handling and/or conduct of inbound tours) to individuals or groups for a fee, commission, or any form of compensation.
Tourism	the all-embracing term for the movement of people

	to destinations away from their place of residence for any reason other than following an occupation, remunerated from within the country visited, for a period of 24 hours or more
Tourism industry	a group of businesses that provide services and facilities for consumption by tourists
Tourism infrastructure	roads, railway lines, harbours, airport runways, water, electricity, other power supplies, sewerage disposal systems and other utilities to serve not only the local residents but also the tourist influx (suitable accommodation, restaurants and passenger transport terminals form the superstructure of the region)
Tourism product	different things to the various members of the tourism industry. To the hotel it is 'guest- nights'. To the airline it is the 'seats flown' and the 'passenger miles'. To the museum, art gallery or archaeological site, the product is measured in terms of the number of visitors. For the tourist the product is the complete experience resulting from the package tour or travel facility purchased, from the time they leave home until their return.
Tourists	people who travel away from home for a range of purposes including travelling for pleasure, entertainment or cultural experiences, for business, to visit friends or family or to attend meetings or conferences for more than 24 hours.
Tourist facility	a feature created for utilization by tourists
Tourist trend	a general tendency to visit a country, region or destination or to pursue a specific tourist activity
Usual Environment	Corresponds to the geographical boundaries within which an individual displaces himself/herself within his/her regular routine of life; consists of the direct vicinity of his/her home and place of work or study and other places frequently visited.
Visitor	Any person traveling to a place other than that of his/her usual environment for less than 12 months and whose main purpose of trip is other than the exercise of an activity remunerated from within the place visited.
World heritage site	a site designated by UNESCO as being of special historical, cultural or natural importance

○ How long will you be gone?   얼마나 가 있을 거예요?
○ How long are you going to stay there?   거기에 얼마나 머무르실 겁니까?

○ It's up in the air for now.   아직 미정입니다.
○ I've not decided yet.   아직 결정하지 않았어요.

○ When are you leaving/ going?   언제 떠나세요?/가세요?
○ When is your departure day/ date?   출발일이 언제에요?

○ What plane/ flight are you taking?   어떤 항공기를 이용하세요?

○ What airline are you booked on?   어떤 항공사에 예약했나요?
○ What airline are you reserved a seat on?   어떤 항공사에 좌석을 예약했나요?

○ I've made an application for a visa to the United States.   미국 비자를 받기 위해서 지원서를 제출했습니다.

○ How did your visa application go?	비자신청은 어떻게 되어가고 있나요?
○ I'd like to make a reservation for a flight to New York.	뉴욕행 항공편을 예약하고 싶습니다.
○ I'll check it for you.	당신을 위해 확인해 드리겠습니다.
○ I'll see what's available.	이용 가능한 것이 있는지 알아보겠습니다.
○ When would you like to leave?	언제 떠나고 싶습니까?
○ Is there a nonstop flight to Boston?	보스턴까지 직항편이 있나요?
○ Where do I change planes to go to Boston?	보스턴으로 가려면 어디서 비행기를 갈 아타야 하나요?
○ Is there a connecting flight from New York to Boston?	뉴욕에서 보스턴으로 가는 연결편이 있 나요?
○ Is there a connection from Chicago to Cincinnati?	시카고에서 신시내티로 가는 연결편이 있나요?
○ How would you like change your reservation?	예약을 어떻게 바꿔 드릴까요?
○ Put me on the waiting list.	대기자 명단에 올려 주세요.
○ I'd like to check in.	체크인 하고 싶습니다.
○ Is this the check-in counter for Korean Airline?	여기가 대한항공의 체크인 카운터인가요?
○ I'd like to check this baggage.	수하물을 맡기고 싶습니다.
○ You must pay for the extra weight.	당신은 초과무게수당을 내야 합니다.
○ Here is your claim tag.	여기 수화물보관증입니다.
○ Can I take this one on with me?	이거 가져가도 되나요?
○ Excuse me, which way is it to Gate 10, please?	실례합니다, 10번 출구는 어느 쪽입니까?
○ Could you direct me to Gate 10, please?	10번 출구로 어떻게 가야 하나요? = How do I get to Gate 10, please?
○ How do I get to Gate 10, please?	
○ How do I fasten this seat belt?	안전벨트를 어떻게 매나요?
○ Would you show me how to fasten	안전벨트를 어떻게 매는지 보여줄 수 있

this seat belt?

○ Will you show me how to buckle this?

○ Just insert the clap/ link into the main buckle.
○ Press this part and pull out.

○ How do I adjust this seat?
○ How do I move my seat back?
○ How can I get the back of my chair to recline?

○ Which way would you like it? Upright or reclined?
○ I want to have it reclined.
○ Just press this button and push the back of the chair backward.

○ May I change my seat?
○ Would you mind trading seats with me?
○ Would you mind exchanging seats, so I can sit with my colleagues.
○ Can I have something to drink?
○ Would you please get me some orange juice?

○ Will there be any movies shown?
○ What movie are we going to see?

○ When will the meal be served?
○ Will dinner be served soon?

○ Would you prefer chicken or beef?

○ Please return your seat to the upright position.

○ Are you through with your meal?
○ How do I fill in this form?

나요?
이 버클을 어떻게 매는지 보여줄 수 있나요?

그냥 클랩/연결쇄를 메인 버클에 넣으세요.
이 부분을 누르고 빼세요.

좌석을 어떻게 조절하나요?
좌석 등받이를 어떻게 뒤로 젖히나요?
어떻게 의자등받이를 눕힐 수 있나요?

어떤 방법이 좋으신가요? 세우는 것 또는 눕히는 것?
저는 눕히고 싶습니다.
그냥 버튼을 누르고 뒤로 의자의 등받이를 미세요.

좌석을 바꿀 수 있나요?
저와 좌석을 바꾸시겠습니까?

제 동료들과 함께 앉을 수 있도록 자리를 바꿔주시겠습니까?
마실 거 있나요?
오렌지 주스 좀 마실 수 있을까요?

상영되는 영화가 있을까요?
어떤 영화를 보게 될까요?

언제 식사가 제공됩니까?
저녁식사는 곧 제공됩니까?

치킨 또는 소고기 어떤 것으로 하시겠어요?

당신의 좌석을 원위치로 세워 주세요.

식사를 끝내셨나요?
이 양식을 어떻게 작성하나요?

- Could you help me with these forms? 이 양식을 작성하는 것을 도와주시겠어요?

- I've filled out these forms and what should I do with them? 이 양식을 다 채우고 나서 이것을 어떻게 해야 하나요?

- How many more hours to go? 몇 시간이나 더 가야 하나요?

- Are we on schedule? 예정대로 진행되고 있나요?

- What's the time difference between Seoul and Los Angeles? 서울과 LA 사이의 시차가 얼마나 됩니까?

- What will the weather be like in Los Angeles? 로스앤젤레스의 날씨는 어떤가요?

- What's the local time in New York? 뉴욕의 현지 시간은 몇 시입니까?

- We'll be landing in an hour. 우리는 한 시간 내에 착륙할 것입니다.

- Can I buy duty-free items on board? 기내에서 면세품을 살 수 있나요?
- Do you have any duty-free items for sale? 면세품을 판매하고 있나요?

- How many bottles of liquor can I carry into the country without having to pay tax? 얼마나 많은 술을 세금을 내지 않고 국내에 가져갈 수 있나요?

- I'm a transit passenger. 나는 통과여객입니다.

- My plane has stopped over at this airport for refueling. 제가 탄 비행기는 연료를 넣기 위해 이 공항에 착륙했어요.
- We're having a layover for our connection to Boston. 우리는 보스턴으로 가는 연결편을 위해 잠시 하차(정거)하고 있습니다.

- Where is your plane bound for? 목적지가 어디입니까?

- How do I know when to board? 언제 탑승하는지 어떻게 알 수 있나요?

- There will be an announcement for boarding. 탑승을 위한 안내방송이 있을 것이다.

- How long do we have to wait for our connecting flight?

연결편(갈아 탈 비행기)을 위해서 얼마나 기다려야 하나요?

- Do you have a return ticket?

돌아가는 편의 티켓이 있나요?

- What's your final destination in the States?

미국에서 당신의 최종 목적지는 어디입니까?

- How much money are you carrying on with you?

당신은 얼마의 돈을 가지고 있습니까?

- Where do I pick up my baggage?

어디에서 내 짐을 찾을 수 있나요?

- I'm looking for a baggage claim area.

저는 짐 찾는 곳을 찾고 있습니다.

- It's right over there, where that carousel is turning.

그것은 바로 저기 수하물 컨베이어 벨트가 돌아가는 곳에 있습니다.

- Do you have anything to declare?

신고할 것이 있습니까?

- I have nothing to declare.

나는 신고할 것이 없습니다.

- Nothing special. Just my personal belongings.

특별한 것은 없습니다. 그냥 개인적인 소지품뿐입니다.

- Please handle it with care. There's something fragile in it.

조심해서 다뤄주세요. 안에 깨지기 쉬운 것이 있습니다.

- I'd like to cash this traveler's check.

이 여행자수표를 현금으로 바꾸고 싶습니다.

- Can I exchange Korean money for U.S. dollars?

한국 돈을 미국 달러로 환전할 수 있을까요?

- What's the exchange rate of won to the dollar?

달러에 대한 원(한국 돈)의 환율은 어떻게 되나요?

- How much would you like to exchange?

얼마만큼 환전하고 싶으세요?

- How would you like the money?

돈은 어떤 걸 원하세요? (지폐? 동전? 이런 뜻인 듯)

- What price range do you have in mind?

어떤 가격대를 생각하고 계시나요?

- I'd like a moderate priced hotel/ economy hotel.

나는 중간정도(moderate) 가격의 호텔을 원합니다/ 저렴한 가격의(economy) 호텔을 원합니다.

○ How often do buses run on this route?	이 노선에서 버스가 얼마나 자주 오나요?
○ What time is the bus for Cincinnati leaving?	신시내티행 버스가 떠나는 시간은 몇 시인가요?
○ At which gate do I get on the bus for Miami?	몇 번 출구에서 마이애미로 가는 버스를 탈 수 있나요?
○ Could you tell me when to get off, please?	언제 내려야 할지 제게 말씀해 주실 수 있나요?
○ I'm sorry. I have to get off ahead of you.	죄송합니다. 저는 당신보다 먼저 내립니다.
○ From which track does my train leave?	어떤 트랙에서 제 기차가 떠나나요?
○ Do I have to make a reservation to take a train?	기차를 타기 위해서 예약을 해야 하나요?
○ Not always. It depends on what train you take.	항상 그런 것은 아닙니다. 그것은 당신이 어떤 기차를 타느냐에 따라 달라요.
○ How long does the return ticket hold good?	이 돌아가는 편의 티켓은 언제까지 유효한가요?
○ The term of validity is written on the ticket.	유효기간은 티켓에 쓰여져 있습니다.
○ What time is there a train to Chicago?	시카고로 가는 기차는 몇 시에 있나요?
○ Every hour on the hour.	매 정시마다 있습니다.
○ How many stops are there on the way to the zoo?	동물원에 가는 길에는 몇 개의 정거장이 있습니까?
○ There are five stops. Get off at the sixth.	5개의 정거장이 있습니다. 6번째에서 내리세요.
○ Is there a drop-off charge for one way?	편도에는 인도 비용1)이 있나요?

---

1) 렌터카를 빌릴 때 빌리는 곳과 돌려주는 곳이 다를 경우 차를 다시 갖다놓는데 드는 비용

○ Do you charge mileage?

○ We offer a free unlimited mileage policy.

○ Do you have vacancies?
○ Do you have a room available?

○ Do you have anything less expensive?
○ I have to stick to my budget.

○ The only thing available at the moment is a suite.

○ May I have a look at the room before I check in?

○ I'd like to change my room.
○ The room is noisy.
○ This room is a little stuffy.

○ What's the rate?
○ What's the charge? What's the cost?

○ How much do you charge for a single room per night?
○ Could you give me a wake-up call tomorrow morning?

○ Will you put it on my hotel bill, please?
○ Will you charge it to my room?

○ Where can I enjoy some local food?
○ Could you suggest a nice place where I can enjoy some local food?
○ Could you recommend a good place where I can eat something special?

○ Will you please reserve a table for five people at seven o'clock today?

주행거리에 따라 요금을 매기나요?

우리는 주행거리에 제한을 두지 않고 따로 요금을 매기지 않는 정책을 시행합니다.

빈 방이 있나요?
사용 가능한 방이 있나요?

덜 비싼 것이 있나요?
나는 예산 내에서 소비를 해야 합니다.

지금 가능한 것은 스위트룸밖에 없습니다.

체크인 하기 전에 방을 먼저 봐도 될까요?

나는 방을 바꾸고 싶습니다.
이 방은 너무 시끄러워요.
이 방은 조금 답답하다.

가격이 얼마입니까?

싱글룸은 하룻밤에 얼마입니까?

내일 아침에 모닝콜을 해주실 수 있으신가요?

제 호텔비에 포함시켜 주실 수 있으신가요?

제 방 값과 함께 청구해 주시겠어요?

어디서 현지 음식을 즐길 수 있을까요?
현지 음식을 즐길 만한 좋은 장소를 추천해 주실 수 있나요?
특별한 것을 먹을 만한 좋은 장소를 추천해 주실 수 있나요?

오늘 7시에 5명이 앉을 자리를 예약해주

- What name do I make it under?

  실 수 있나요?
  누구 이름으로 예약해 드릴까요?

- Is it necessary to make a reservation in advance to dine at your restaurant?

  당신의 레스토랑에서 식사를 하려면 미리 예약해두는 것이 필요할까요?

- Is formal dress required?

  정장(격식 있는 옷)을 입어야 하나요?

- What's good here?
- What's today's special?
- Do you have anything special today?
- What do you have for today's special?

  여기서 뭐가 맛있나요?
  오늘 특별메뉴는 무엇인가요?
  오늘 특별한 메뉴가 있나요?
  오늘 특별한 메뉴로는 어떤 것이 있나요?

- Would you like to order?
- Are you ready to order?
- May I take your order?

  주문하시겠습니까?

- How would you like your steak?
- How do you want your steak?

  스테이크는 어떻게 요리해 드릴까요?

- Would like it well-done?

  웰던으로 해드릴까요?

- I don't think this is what I ordered. This is not what I ordered.
- I didn't ask for this.

  제가 주문한 것은 이것이 아닙니다.

- This is not my order.

  제가 주문한 것은 이것이 아닙니다.

- My order hasn't come yet.
- It will be coming out in a minute.

  제가 주문한 것이 아직 안 나왔어요.
  곧 나올 것입니다.

- Where do I pay the bill?
- Do I pay you or the cashier?

  어디서 계산하나요?
  당신에게 계산하면 되나요 아니면 계산대에서 계산하나요?

- Does this bill include the service charge?

  이 계산서에는 서비스료가 포함되어 있는 것인가요?

- Is this with or without tax?

  이것은 세금 포함 가격인가요 아닌가요?

저자약력

이승재

이화여자대학교 영어영문학과 졸업
이화여자대학교 대학원 석/박사
George Washington University, Master of Tourism Administration 수료
Certificate of Teaching English as a Second Language (UCSD)
University of California, San Diego, Visiting Scholar
Univeristy of North Carolina, Chapel Hill, Adjunct Professor
한국외국어대학교 통역번역대학원 BK21 선임연구원
경희대학교 호텔관광대학 조교수

저자와의
합의하에
인지첩부
생략

An Introduction to Culture and Tourism

2015년 3월 5일 초 판 1쇄 발행
2017년 8월 25일 제2판 1쇄 발행
2024년 4월 5일 제2판 2쇄 발행

지은이 이승재
펴낸이 진욱상
펴낸곳 백산출판사
교 정 편집부
본문디자인 오행복
표지디자인 오정은

등 록 1974년 1월 9일 제406-1974-000001호
주 소 경기도 파주시 회동길 370(백산빌딩 3층)
전 화 02-914-1621(代)
팩 스 031-955-9911
이메일 edit@ibaeksan.kr
홈페이지 www.ibaeksan.kr

ISBN 979-11-5763-036-3
값 15,000원